Amazing BIBLE WORD SEARCHES for Kids

Richard & Ruth Spiering

HARVEST HOUSE PUBLISHERS

EUGENE, OREGON

Unless otherwise indicated, all Scripture quotations are taken from the HOLY BIBLE, NEW INTER-NATIONAL VERSION ®. NIV®. Copyright © 1973, 1978, 1984 by the International Bible Society. Used by permission of Zondervan. All rights reserved.

Verses marked KJV are taken from the King James Version of the Bible.

Verses marked NKJV are taken from the New King James Version. Copyright © 1982 by Thomas Nelson, Inc. Used by permission. All rights reserved.

Verses marked DARBY are taken from the Darby version of the Bible.

Cover design and illustrations by Katie Brady Design, Eugene, Oregon

---

We acknowledge...

Terry Glaspey, who is so wonderfully enthusiastic

Barb Gordon, a great editor who keeps yummies at her desk for us to munch on

Betty Fletcher and Laura Knudson, dear editorial buddies par excellence—hugs to you

Especially Gary Lineburg, Design & Layout master, without whose expertise our books would not be in print

Always and ever, our Lord Jesus Christ, Savior and Keeper, to whom all Scripture points

> *"Trust in the LORD with all your heart, and lean not*
> *on your own understanding; in all your ways*
> *acknowledge Him, and He shall direct your paths."*
> PROVERBS 3:5-6 NKJV

AMAZING BIBLE WORD SEARCHES FOR KIDS
Copyright © 2004 by Richard and Ruth Spiering
Published 2011 by Harvest House Publishers
Eugene, Oregon 97408
www.harvesthousepublishers.com

ISBN 978-0-7369-2961-5

Printed in the United States of America

20 21 22 23 24 / B P- K B / 10 9 8

Contents

Hints to Make
Word Searches More Fun

- Choose two different-colored pens or pencils. Work the Word Search with one of them.

- Write words and draw lines as neatly as you can.

- For best results try to find the longest words first.

- When you find a word in the Word Search from the *word list,* (circle) the whole word (see Sample Word Searches A and B on page 7). Then underline, ~~line out~~, or check off (✓) that same word in the list.

- Words will be horizontal (◄—►) or vertical (↕), forward (—►) or backward (◄—), or diagonal (↘ ↙).

- Be sure to read any "Hint," "Find," and/or "Clue" printed below a Word Search.

- Words may cross each other and share letters.

More Hints:

- *Scripture-text* Word Searches may use **ALL-CAPS**, **BOLDFACE** words, or every word in the scripture.

- *Underlined* words **APPEAR TOGETHER** in a Word Search.

- *Blank lines* on some Word Searches are for you to fill in. Look up the answers in your New International Version Bible.

- *Hidden message* notation in a Word Search will say: Find: [#]-word hidden message. Use your second colored pen or pencil to (circle) or underline the unused letters. Begin at the top left corner of the puzzle, as you would read a book (see Sample Word Search B). Then write down the letters to read the message.

☞ Are you having trouble finding the diagonal words? (See Sample Word Searches.) Lay a 6" ruler down on the diagonal rows and move it from line to line. (You may use the ruler with the straight across and up-and-down letters, too, if you want to.)

☞ When you read the verses, ask yourself, "What is God saying to me?"

Moms and Dads:

Are you curious about why a word was used or wonder about its context? You will find the Scripture reference in the index of Scripture References for Word-List Word Searches at the back of the book on p. 169. You may want to help your child do the more challenging Word Searches.

Remember:

The Bible is God's Word to us.

☞ It was written to teach us.   Romans 15:4

☞ It is profitable to us.   2 Timothy 3:16-17 KJV

☞ It is sharper than a double-edged sword.   Hebrews 4:12

☞ We are to study it to be approved of God.   2 Timothy 2:15

☞ There is a blessing for those who read it.   Revelation 1:3

☞ God's Word is truth.   John 17:17

Amazing Bible Word Searches for Kids

 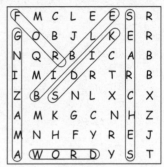

Find these words: Amazing Bible word searches for kids

Clue: (Circle) the letters in the puzzle to mark each word that you have found.

Hint: Words are horizontal, vertical, and diagonal.

Word Search with a Hidden Message

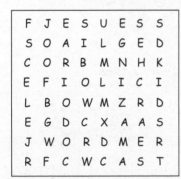 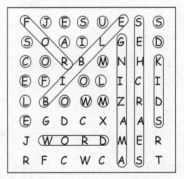

Find these words: Amazing Bible word searches for kids

Clue: Words are horizontal, vertical, and diagonal.

Find the hidden message: After you have completed the Word Search, begin at the top left corner of the puzzle and (circle) each unused letter to find an important 5-word message. Write all the letters in order on the line below to read the message:

<u>Jesus said Come follow Me</u>

1

Jesus and the Word

Word Search No. 1

No Other Savior

```
T  H  H  C  I  H  W  G  E  I  S  I  S
T  H  H  E  D  A  Y  I  S  R  T  H  E
U  N  D  E  R  L  O  V  U  D  E  R  D
H  A  S  M  A  A  D  E  S  E  E  H  L
E  T  U  S  R  V  E  N  E  A  J  S  T
D  N  U  O  F  O  E  R  J  D  A  I  C
R  E  A  N  D  T  B  N  A  L  E  G  L
E  A  D  I  S  N  M  D  V  I  E  I  T
H  W  Y  I  T  E  D  A  E  M  S  L  V
T  B  R  T  N  S  T  N  A  V  F  E  R
O  H  J  W  Z  I  U  N  X  X  A  N  D
C  C  T  R  O  K  V  M  Y  D  Z  S  T
R  K  B  N  D  N  A  Z  A  R  E  T  H
```

Hint: Words are horizontal, vertical, and diagonal.
Find: 16-word hidden message.

"**JESUS CHRIST** of **NAZARETH**…God **RAISED** from the **DEAD**… **SALVATION** is **FOUND** in no one else, for **THERE** is no **OTHER NAME UNDER HEAVEN GIVEN** to **MEN** by **WHICH** we **MUST** be **SAVED**."

—Acts 4:10,12

Word Search No. 2

New Testament Books

```
C O R I N T H I A N S I I R P T Z J
T S J T I V H X J O H N I I N L N N
H C E O K I I Y H T O M I T S R S K
E P O M H D Y K R A M Q Z N T X N H
S X E R A N T H T P N X A Y C Q A M
S P P Q I J I I T Y M I L J A M I G
A I H W N N T K Y O S Y P U T K P Q
L I E J E U T F Y S M P F D D G P I
O R S R S H N H O D I I T E A D I J
N E I D O M T L I R M R T L D I L K
I T A B R M O T E A L R A G N K I Y
A E N D T C A T A N N T Y H H R H N
N P S D Y P E N N M I S O L O V P R
S M B G C P J L S A K J I Z J H Q K
I K I I S N A I N O L A S S E H T L
V M K H P Y P S W B T R C H B L U W
R S W E R B E H M T J J D F Q K Q W
P H I L E M O N N O I T A L E V E R
```

Hint: Words are horizontal, vertical, and diagonal.

___ Acts	___ John III	___ Philemon
___ Colossians	___ John II	___ Philippians
___ Corinthians II	___ John I	___ Revelation
___ Corinthians I	___ Jude	___ Romans
___ Ephesians	___ Luke	___ Thessalonians II
___ Galatians	___ Mark	___ Thessalonians I
___ Hebrews	___ Matthew	___ Timothy II
___ James	___ Peter II	___ Timothy I
___ John	___ Peter I	___ Titus

Please number the books in their proper Bible order (1-27).

Word Search No. 3

Precious Things in Scripture

```
Y  E  O  U  J  A  R  S  T  H  G  U  O  H  T  E
E  N  U  P  A  S  E  R  I  H  P  P  A  S  R  E
N  O  O  C  C  S  I  E  F  I  L  O  U  S  T  O
O  T  Y  T  O  E  H  E  M  O  D  S  I  W  L  O
T  S  R  D  B  I  J  E  S  S  T  O  N  E  S  P
S  G  U  E  S  B  X  O  W  N  P  M  Y  M  E  E
S  N  M  Z  G  U  Y  I  D  R  X  M  W  F  C  A
I  I  V  N  Z  R  Z  L  E  D  O  O  L  B  A  R
H  V  V  O  G  O  L  D  W  W  G  F  X  D  F  L
T  I  N  R  R  K  D  I  S  R  A  E  L  E  T  S
T  L  M  B  N  K  V  V  Y  O  Y  L  K  R  A  L  V
H  E  N  O  T  S  R  E  N  R  O  C  K  T  Y  T
I  G  L  J  Q  Q  K  G  Y  V  R  F  N  H  Y  F
N  L  A  W  K  H  L  T  X  K  L  E  W  E  J  I
G  Q  V  W  W  Y  K  S  O  N  S  T  G  R  R  G
S  Z  K  P  R  O  M  I  S  E  S  F  A  I  T  H
```

Find: 7-word hidden message.

blood	Jacob	sapphires
bronze	jewel	sons
cornerstone	law	stones
death	life	things
dew	living Stone	this stone
face	oil	thoughts
faith	onyx	wisdom
gift	pearls	you
gold	promises	
Israel	rubies	

The First Miracle of Jesus

"On the third day a **WEDDING** took place at **CANA** in **GALILEE**. Jesus' **MOTHER** was there, and Jesus and his **DISCIPLES** had also been **INVITED** to the wedding.

"When the **WINE** was gone, Jesus' mother said to him, 'They have no more wine.'

" 'Dear **WOMAN**, why do you **INVOLVE** me?' Jesus replied. 'My time has not yet come.'

"His mother said to the servants, 'Do **WHATEVER** he tells you.'

"**NEARBY** stood six **STONE** water **JARS**, the kind used by the Jews for **CEREMONIAL WASHING**, each **HOLDING** from **TWENTY** to **THIRTY GALLONS**.

"Jesus said to the servants, 'Fill the jars with **WATER**'; so they **FILLED** them to the brim. Then he told them, 'Now **DRAW** some out and take it to the **MASTER** of the **BANQUET**.'

"They did so, and the master of the banquet **TASTED** the water that had been **TURNED** into wine. He did not **REALIZE** where it had come from, though the **SERVANTS** who had drawn the water knew. Then he called the **BRIDEGROOM** aside and said, '**EVERYONE** brings out the choice wine first and then the **CHEAPER** wine after the guests have had too much to drink; but you have **SAVED** the best till now.'

"This, the first of his **MIRACULOUS** signs, Jesus **PERFORMED** at Cana in Galilee. He thus **REVEALED** his **GLORY**, and his disciples put their **FAITH** in him."

—John 2:1-11

Word Search No. 4

The First Miracle of Jesus

```
N Z G Y J T N E A R B Y G A L L O N S T
B D D R C E V K F R E A L I Z E P D B X
R I E Z Y V G N I H S A W N W B B L M N
I S T G N L L S G A L I L E E Y L T H D
D C S N Q O V K T B K F J E N I W G G F
E I A V Z V Y N G O C R E P A E H C A I
G P T D Y N J N N D N R E T S A M N G L
R L B T E I C L I W K E C N B W A C F L
O E L L M V N V D K W T N N K C A C X E
O S B J Y O A T D W P S W A G Y Z T F D
M S K A T L T S E N G N E C M N D D E G
P U T R N Q L H W U N N E R H O E C E R
E O T S E J G N E D Q R I I V N W V P R
R L P R W L Y Y D R E N N D R A E T E E
F U N B T R T R D M M V A U L R N V N V
O C K F O R A M O G I R T B Y O E T T E
R A G L I W N N L T K K C O X T H B S A
M R G H Q C I K E Y C L N F A I T H K L
E I T Z M A H D R T J E Q H N R Q K D E
D M R X L P X H H Z F J W D D K F B J D
```

Hint: Words are horizontal, vertical, and diagonal.

Word Search No. 5

Jesus

```
K K K D T Q W S M J E S U S C Y N R R V
J L J E S U S S U S F S U S E J K L Z R
K E E R F U H U U S F Z U R J T E Z N W
J E S U S K S S V U E Z T S J E H S J S
T V U U M W E E M S H J Q Z E E S E U U
Y M S H S J K J J E J K J D S J S U L S
J E S U S Y E S E J W E P T U U Q U S E
J E S U S S U S K S S W S L S S S Y S J
H E Y M U S U Q Z U U P W U S U S E J D
J K N S E S N J S J E S U S S S S R J S
Z H J J E S E D S J J M S U S E J E N U
M J E J E S U U E J F E T R V J S K J S
J E S K U S S S M T J Y S X S U S E J E
E S U S J E U C E E J S S U S S U S E J
S U S W J S J S S J U U S J S S S J B J
U S M H J J E U E S S E B Y K U S E S E
S S U S E J S S E E J U L M S S U S U S
G J E S U S U J J X S U S E J E S U S U
R M U L E S S P S U S E J E P J E S E S
T S Q M P J E S U S W T C P J F J B J K
```

Hint: Words are horizontal, vertical, and diagonal.

Find all the occurrences of the name "Jesus" in the Word Search.

"**JESUS** answered, 'I am the way and the truth and the life. No one comes to the Father except through me'" (John 14:6).

How many times does it appear in the puzzle? _____

Clue: the number of books in the Bible _____

Each time you find and circle the word "Jesus," make a hash mark (/) at the bottom of this page to help you in your counting.

Word Search No. 6

Old Testament Books: History/Poetry

```
H  I  P  R  P  Q  B  Z  Q  L  Y  J  F  N  N  X  P  J
R  S  S  R  P  R  K  H  G  R  O  I  L  E  U  M  A  S
I  E  A  T  O  M  G  B  S  B  T  I  Q  X  G  X  T  N
S  L  L  C  W  V  P  L  T  E  I  C  W  Z  E  N  T  D
G  C  M  B  M  F  E  M  D  S  G  T  V  N  Z  V  M  I
N  I  S  T  G  N  Y  R  E  B  Q  D  N  G  R  X  I  D
I  N  Y  M  R  Y  N  L  B  H  C  T  U  R  A  S  W  H
K  O  M  Z  L  X  C  Y  P  S  Y  E  X  J  G  K  Q  S
P  R  R  C  V  I  J  Q  K  J  T  M  S  N  M  Y  Q  G
B  H  X  K  N  A  U  H  S  O  J  K  I  T  C  C  M  N
I  C  T  O  G  R  T  V  W  L  G  K  M  H  H  K  B  O
L  I  R  L  U  N  M  T  F  Q  L  K  H  N  D  E  R  S
Y  H  L  T  M  F  R  G  L  H  G  Z  D  D  J  F  R  F
C  B  H  E  C  C  L  E  S  I  A  S  T  E  S  N  T  O
L  T  F  F  U  M  M  N  E  H  E  M  I  A  H  T  Z  G
R  L  F  X  D  M  P  B  X  J  T  Z  G  G  B  V  Y  N
C  W  H  H  N  T  A  F  C  L  L  K  R  R  Y  P  D  O
L  Y  T  L  M  K  F  S  Z  M  V  V  C  G  C  J  T  S
```

Hint: Words are horizontal, vertical, and diagonal.

___ Chronicles I	___ Kings I
___ Chronicles II	___ Kings II
___ Ecclesiastes	___ Nehemiah
___ Esther	___ Proverbs
___ Ezra	___ Psalms
___ Job	___ Ruth
___ Joshua	___ Samuel I
___ Judges	___ Samuel II
	___ Song of Songs

Please number the books in their proper Bible order (1-17).

I AM's of Jesus in John 10-20

10:7   I AM: "the _____ for the _____."

10:11   I AM: "the good _____."

11:25   I AM: "the _____ and the life."

12:26   "Where I AM, my _____ also will be."

13:13   "_____ and _____...is what I AM."

13:19   I AM: "_____ you...I AM He."

14:2   I AM: going "to _____ a place for you."

14:3   "You also may be _____ I AM."

14:6   I AM: "the _____ and the _____ and the _____."

14:11   I AM: "in the _____."

14:12   I AM: "_____ to the Father."

15:1   I AM: "the _____ _____."

16:5   I AM: "going to him who _____ me."

16:28   I AM: "_____ the world."

18:37   I AM: "a _____."

19:28   I AM: "_____."

20:17   I AM: "_____ to my Father."

20:21   I AM: "_____ you."

Word Search No. 7

I AM's of Jesus in John 10-20

```
B  W  R  K  P  G  L  T  G  N  I  L  L  E  T
Q  W  R  R  L  R  T  H  G  N  I  O  G  V  R
P  X  H  M  Y  N  K  I  Y  E  L  V  Z  T  E
E  D  Q  A  E  T  X  R  N  R  I  R  F  E  T
T  R  W  S  Y  M  J  S  F  E  F  H  F  A  U
M  R  A  R  M  H  E  T  V  H  E  A  P  C  R
W  C  U  P  W  T  T  Y  T  W  T  E  K  H  N
S  N  E  T  E  M  A  G  M  H  E  L  R  E  I
R  E  M  U  H  R  G  X  E  H  X  K  L  R  N
E  B  R  K  R  Y  P  R  S  W  Q  L  I  G  G
N  C  H  V  J  T  K  L  T  L  L  J  Q  N  B
I  Q  D  L  A  L  S  H  E  P  H  E  R  D  G
V  V  O  T  Y  N  R  X  L  E  A  V  I  N  G
H  R  L  N  T  B  T  W  S  E  N  D  I  N  G
D  R  E  S  U  R  R  E  C  T  I  O  N  W  R
```

Hints: Words are horizontal, vertical, and diagonal.
Words do not cross or share letters.

Word Search No. 8

Jesus Heals Bartimaeus

S	L	Y	L	E	T	A	I	D	E	M	M	I	O	O	K
U	I	N	G	J	U	M	P	E	D	U	N	T	O	J	E
E	L	S	U	S	T	H	D	E	P	P	O	T	S	D	E
A	E	D	I	S	C	I	P	L	E	S	A	U	T	W	H
M	A	O	R	A	N	C	A	L	L	I	N	G	Y	O	U
I	V	O	T	R	D	Y	S	U	E	A	M	I	T	R	F
T	I	H	E	E	I	C	F	N	I	S	H	E	R	C	O
R	N	C	E	C	F	R	A	T	H	R	O	W	I	N	G
A	G	I	F	E	O	E	I	U	D	A	O	R	R	F	A
B	C	R	R	I	I	M	T	D	E	W	O	L	L	O	F
T	H	E	U	V	H	E	H	T	H	S	I	G	H	T	V
U	E	J	O	E	E	V	H	T	E	R	A	Z	A	N	R
O	E	W	Y	D	A	A	D	G	C	R	A	B	B	I	N
H	R	H	N	J	R	H	V	K	Z	H	E	A	L	E	D
S	U	A	O	L	D	X	D	E	D	I	S	D	A	O	R
V	P	T	B	T	T	D	C	K	A	O	L	C	W	L	L

Find: 10-word hidden message.

"As Jesus and his **DISCIPLES**, together with a large **CROWD**, were **LEAVING** [**JERICHO**], a blind man, **BARTIMAEUS** (…Son of **TIMAEUS**), was sitting by the **ROADSIDE** begging. When he **HEARD** that it was Jesus of **NAZARETH**, he began to **SHOUT**, 'Jesus, Son of David, **HAVE MERCY** on me!'…

"Jesus **STOPPED** and said, 'Call him.' So they called to the blind man, '**CHEER UP**! **ON YOUR FEET**! He's **CALLING YOU**.'

"**THROWING** his **CLOAK** aside, he **JUMPED** to his feet and came to Jesus.

"'**WHAT** do you want me to do for you?' Jesus asked him. The blind man said, '**RABBI**, I want to see.'

"'Go,' said Jesus, 'your **FAITH** has **HEALED** you.' **IMMEDIATELY** he **RECEIVED** his **SIGHT** and **FOLLOWED** Jesus along the **ROAD**."

—Mark 10:46-47,49-52

Word Search No. 9

All Scripture

```
S  S  E  N  S  U  O  E  T  H  G  I  R
L  E  T  J  Y  K  R  O  W  E  S  U  S
C  O  E  M  L  E  G  I  N  U  T  O  Y
O  U  R  R  H  H  O  E  A  S  R  T  R
T  J  U  C  G  V  O  W  N  E  T  C  C
R  G  T  Q  U  M  D  H  Z  F  D  R  Z
A  N  P  M  O  K  J  C  J  U  N  R  R
I  I  I  H  R  M  N  R  J  L  K  H  B
N  K  R  C  O  R  R  E  C  T  I  N  G
I  U  C  F  H  G  N  I  H  C  A  E  T
N  B  S  G  T  N  P  Z  P  W  Z  M  G
G  E  G  O  D  B  R  E  A  T  H  E  D
L  R  J  E  Q  U  I  P  P  E  D  L  P
```

Find: 6-word hidden message.

"All **SCRIPTURE** is <u>**GOD-BREATHED**</u> and is **USEFUL** for **TEACHING**, **REBUKING**, **CORRECTING** and **TRAINING** in **RIGHTEOUSNESS**, so that the man of God may be **THOROUGHLY EQUIPPED** for every **GOOD WORK**."

—2 Timothy 3:16-17

Bible Facts

Try to answer these questions from memory. If in doubt, search the Scriptures.

1. The first man to set foot on earth _____

2. God's words are written in the _____

3. The giant slayer _____

4. The very first mother on earth _____

5. The writer of the Gospel of John _____

6. The mother of Jesus _____

7. The baby in the floating basket _____

8. The builder of the floating ark _____

9. A man known for his physical strength _____

10. The number of books in the Old Testament _____

11. The number of books in the New Testament _____

12. The number of chapters in Genesis _____

13. The number of chapters in Ruth _____

14. The number of chapters in Proverbs _____

15. The number of chapters in Acts _____

16. The man in the lions' den _____

17. Jesus walked on water, and so did _____

18. A book of the Bible named after a queen _____

19. King David's wisest son _____

20. The man who betrayed Jesus for money _____

Word Search No. 10
Bible Facts

```
T W E N T Y S E V E N T F O R E
Z S E S O M R R A H H A D D E V
O T E D H I M S E I E N L F T O
D A V I D T H E R T O S T U E T
D Y A N D M O T B M E S E N N W
R V A N A C Y E O H O P I F O E
T H E R L O J L A W A N O R S N
F T Y H N E O L O R Y O D E M T
A N D E T S H O T T E A N H A Y
C M H I N G N I R T S D E T S E
C A R E E S A I N D L F E S A I
W D S I N I H S R A E L I E L G
E A Z R A T S F E V B E N F T H
E N E J C G M O J I R R J Q T T
K G P V V M L U B L E I N A D Y
Z H L W E Z W R J U D A S B R Z
```

Hint: Words are horizontal, vertical, and diagonal.
Find: 28-word hidden message.

Word Search No. 11

Names and Titles of Christ

```
B G R A T S G N I N R O M T H G I R B G F H
L H C L G G B R T M K F T J Q F M R S J P T
E N O N B M R Y J Y W Q F R F Q Z S T J B C
S M V N P E T X N R R J L P M L E D G T J R
S T E R V N G N D D Z R H C Q N L D Z G H Y
E H N O M O M I M M Z N L F T L B R R M P V
D G A L H D T W N G O H K I R A U T H O R H
A I N E P E H B N N O W J N K E Y J N B T
N L T S Z T J R V K I L R L R L Z C Z R M K
D G F N B N V Q X J U N F G T D T V A L T B
O N O U Y I G X B F B T G S E Y N N H Q R Z
N I R O Q O H L H N R K O A N D C K T Y F D
L T T C T N K T Q T T P T M N H I G P T T B
Y S H L T A I T X Z A X N R P D M R L Z V J
R A E B H A T K Z T Y W K Q G F T Q B Q G V
U L P F F N Q H R X M X R V F F Y H K F K X
L R E F I L F O D A E R B K H B N J E N X Z
E E O R W F A I T H F U L A N D T R U E T G
R V P B K R Z L T D P W B W B P K M H B N N
H E L Q T H R P Q L R Y N K Y M K X C F X D
E V E R L A S T I N G F A T H E R Q R R W N
F A I T H F U L A N D T R U E W I T N E S S
```

Hint: Words are horizontal, vertical, and diagonal.

Anointed One	bright Morning Star
apostle	Counselor
author	Covenant for the people
Beginning and the End	Everlasting Father
blessed and only Ruler	everlasting light
Branch	Faithful and True
bread of life	faithful and true witness
bridegroom	faithful witness

Word Search No. 12

Scrambled Scriptures

```
D  H  M  N  S  G  N  O  S  F  O  G  N  O  S
R  O  U  U  X  H  A  I  N  A  H  P  E  Z  N
H  S  H  M  B  P  D  H  A  I  M  E  R  E  J
D  E  A  B  C  K  Q  K  I  J  G  N  S  S  V
V  A  N  E  J  D  G  Z  T  O  M  M  T  N  L
H  E  B  R  E  W  S  T  A  S  A  Y  C  O  P
B  J  R  S  K  Z  M  M  L  H  L  Q  A  I  P
O  N  Y  A  M  O  S  L  A  U  A  D  T  T  E
J  N  T  W  X  G  W  M  G  A  C  T  N  A  X
D  S  N  A  I  P  P  I  L  I  H  P  L  T  O
H  W  E  H  T  T  A  M  B  Z  I  B  Y  N  D
T  J  N  S  B  R  E  V  O  R  P  K  H  E  U
U  T  J  O  N  A  H  T  V  F  M  N  T  M  S
R  F  N  X  F  L  U  K  E  E  D  U  J  A  R
T  I  T  U  S  N  E  H  E  M  I  A  H  L  T
```

Can you find 24 books of the Bible in this Word Search?

Please write the names of the books below.

Word Search No. 13

Miraculous Signs

```
G  N  I  V  E  I  L  E  B  I  N  S  A  L
L  Y  S  O  U  R  W  A  Y  S  Y  U  A  C
K  N  E  O  N  W  L  G  E  N  Y  S  D  G
E  H  L  E  P  E  O  I  A  A  M  E  A  N
D  H  P  M  R  D  T  M  M  B  E  J  W  I
L  L  I  A  E  M  A  T  O  K  E  Y  O  U
R  P  C  N  S  A  S  O  I  T  H  S  S  T
R  A  S  I  E  G  K  I  C  R  H  T  P  R
O  V  I  E  N  F  R  B  G  H  W  S  T  H
R  E  D  E  C  S  I  I  X  N  R  X  N  R
G  S  T  B  E  R  L  L  F  G  S  I  B  R
N  O  M  I  R  A  C  U  L  O  U  S  S  Q
J  N  X  Q  H  C  B  E  L  I  E  V  E  T
M  W  D  E  D  R  O  C  E  R  V  K  Z  L
```

Hint: Words are horizontal, vertical, and diagonal.

Find: 16-word hidden message.

"**JESUS** did **MANY** other **MIRACULOUS SIGNS** in the **PRESENCE** of his **DISCIPLES**, which are not **RECORDED** in this **BOOK**. But these are **WRITTEN** that you **MAY BELIEVE** that Jesus is the **CHRIST**, the **SON** of **GOD**, and that by **BELIEVING** you may have **LIFE** in his **NAME**."

—John 20:30-31

Word Search No. 14

Scripture Challenge

```
G K S S C R I P T U R E M E R U T P I R C S K Q
R L F C E V P E D Z M S E M E E R U T P I R C S
S M S L R R T L R N Y R C R E R U T P I R C S T
C S V C G I U C M U U E U R E R U T P I R C S T
R S C L R R P T P T T T R E I J K T V B P R L X
I C L R K I M T P M P P X U R P M F P N T M Y D
P R S K I R P I U I Z T I G T U T Y C I D R M E
T I W C X P R T R R R S C R I P T U R E R M Q R
U P L S R C T C U S E C T P C W I P R R M C H U
R T P C S I S U C R F C S X V S T R I E K P S T
E U Y R J F P R R R E C E E E E E C R S N Q P
V R M I B R I T T E R S R R R R R D K S C V K I
S E L P L P L L U I C U U U U U S S E E R S N R
C D G T T R X Y P R T L T T T T C C R R I S S C
R Q E U P J Q T I P E S P P P P R R U U P C C S
I K R R T Q U P I D C I I I I I I T T R R S
P E U E T R T R L R R R R R R P P P P U I I C
T H T K E U C T I C C D C C C C T T I I R P P R
U K P L R S T P S S R T S S S S U U R R E T T I
R T I E T L T S C R I P T U R E R R C C T U U P
E X R Y F U F S C R I P T U R E E E S S J R R T
Y J C E R U T P I R C S S C R I P T U R E E E U
Q N S E D Z M V R W S C R I P T U R E H K T N R
Y L P H E R U T P I R C S E R U T P I R C S H E
```

Hint: Words are horizontal, vertical, and diagonal.

From the verse below look only for the word "Scripture" in the Word Search.

"Does not the **SCRIPTURE** say that the Christ will come from David's family and from Bethlehem, the town where David lived?"

—John 7:42

How many times does it appear? _____

Clue: the number in each group mentioned in Luke 9:14

Each time you find and circle the word "Scripture," make a hash mark (/) at the bottom of this page to help you in your counting.

Son of Man

"Jesus replied, '**FOXES** have holes and **BIRDS** of the air have nests, but the Son of Man has no place to lay his head.'"

—Matthew 8:20

"As Jonah was **THREE DAYS** and three nights in the **BELLY** of a huge fish, so the Son of Man will be three days and three nights in the heart of the **EARTH**."

—Matthew 12:40

"As they were coming down the **MOUNTAIN**, Jesus **INSTRUCTED** them, 'Don't tell anyone what you have seen, until the Son of Man has been **RAISED** from the dead.'"

—Matthew 17:9

"When they came together in **GALILEE** he said to them,…'The Son of Man will be **BETRAYED** to the chief priests and the teachers of the law. They will **CONDEMN** him to death.'"

—Matthew 17:22; 20:18

"The Son of Man did not come to be served, but **TO SERVE**, and to give his life as a **RANSOM** for many."

—Matthew 20:28

"All the nations of the earth will…see the Son of Man coming on the **CLOUDS** of the sky, with **POWER** and great glory."

—Matthew 24:30

"**AS IT WAS** in the days of Noah, **SO IT WILL BE** at the coming of the Son of Man."

—Matthew 24:37

"They **KNEW NOTHING** about what would happen until the **FLOOD** came and took them all away. That is how it will be at the coming of the Son of Man."

—Matthew 24:39

"When the Son of Man comes in his **GLORY**, and all the **ANGELS** with him, he will sit on his **THRONE** in heavenly glory."

—Matthew 25:31

Word Search No. 15

Son of Man

```
T H C X V L Q E V R E S O T R X B
D D M T K Q V T Q L C L O U D S X
Z N L C K L Q S Y A D E E R H T N
G H C M O U N T A I N V N K D N M
I V X L J T X H B E T R A Y E D O
N T Z S O I T W I L L B E Y W R S
S T T Y P L N R N Q H E J K Z B N
T N F D O O L F Z R T L L N P D A
R Y Q D E S I A R T R L Z E O T R
U T H R O N E B S F A Y C W W H K
C B I R D S E N L Y E M O N E S M
T N Q C G R E S E V C M N O R A Y
E L T M T M L E G G H B D T T W T
D B R T P F I X N L V W E H J T D
T K D T N Q L O A M M N M I Q I Y
N R G G Z N A F L R B Z N N L S M
J Y Q X Z G G B Z Y R O L G Z A L
```

Word Search No. 16

1 John 1–2

```
S L I N T H G E C B E G I N D
N K I I N G N G O O D C R L L
E A A G T E I D N T H E R H A
E A V E H E N N F S A O N P N
D T H E P T N E E A W G I R R
T Y H H E S I A S L N H F C E
S D O M A D G E S I S A H T T
H O E S T A E R T W I I S Q E
F B T V Z T B N O T L T M Z N
F Y M C Q C I L H D L M W K N
G N L H P O L F R J R J N L D
D A Q T N E U E M E S S A G E
D N Z A F L N Y M H G H M J D
Q D A N Y T H I N G J Y T M H
S S E N S U O E T H G I R N U
```

Hint: Words are horizontal, vertical, and diagonal.

Find: 15-word hidden message.

1:1 "That which was from the _____"

1:3 "Our _____ is with the Father"

1:5 "This is the _____"

1:7 "if we walk in the _____"

1:9 "if we _____ our sins he is _____ and just and will...purify us from all _____"

2:1 "My dear _____ ...if _____ does sin we have one who _____ to the Father"

2:15 "Do not love the _____ or _____ in the world"

2:20 "you have an _____"

2:25 "he promised us—..._____ life"

Word Search No. 17

Old Testament Books: Prophets

```
N  J  Z  T  K  L  E  I  K  E  Z  E  Z  H  M  M
S  N  O  I  T  A  T  N  E  M  A  L  D  T  V  M
Z  F  H  D  N  T  R  H  A  G  G  A  I  N  F  K
J  E  L  O  K  Z  E  C  H  A  R  I  A  H  X  C
L  D  P  N  S  C  V  B  K  L  Z  J  R  T  L  N
S  E  X  H  T  E  J  R  H  G  E  M  K  W  V  I
O  M  I  R  A  V  A  A  J  R  J  U  P  N  M  S
M  U  D  N  C  N  I  Z  E  O  K  M  Z  H  T  A
A  H  R  X  A  D  I  M  N  K  F  M  W  V  Z  I
K  A  B  T  A  D  I  A  A  X  L  F  N  L  G  A
D  N  N  B  T  A  H  B  H  R  J  W  C  G  T  H
B  R  O  L  H  J  A  A  M  C  O  M  G  C  R  F
H  N  Z  D  P  H  H  M  C  W  E  P  M  N  V  J
B  R  Q  M  Y  F  G  M  K  I  L  K  Q  X  H  V
C  Y  H  N  M  M  J  Z  J  H  M  D  C  F  J  X
R  N  J  F  I  H  C  A  L  A  M  G  T  J  K  G
```

Hint: Words are horizontal, vertical, and diagonal.

Major Prophets

____ Daniel   ____ Isaiah
____ Ezekiel   ____ Jeremiah   ____ Lamentations

Minor Prophets

____ Amos   ____ Joel   ____ Nahum
____ Habakkuk   ____ Jonah   ____ Obadiah
____ Haggai   ____ Malachi   ____ Zechariah
____ Hosea   ____ Micah   ____ Zephaniah

Please number the books in their proper Bible order (1-17).

Word Search No. 18

Eternal Son of God

```
D  T  O  N  L  L  A  H  S  O  Y
O  U  B  E  L  I  E  V  E  S  K
R  N  G  N  I  N  N  I  G  E  B
E  H  D  O  F  H  A  V  E  W  T
V  I  O  H  E  A  T  E  V  A  G
E  M  G  L  O  V  E  D  W  J  H
O  W  E  S  U  N  S  L  O  O  S
H  O  V  E  S  O  Y  O  R  U  I
W  R  W  L  R  S  D  W  L  D  R
Q  D  O  G  H  T  I  W  D  P  E
T  F  E  T  E  R  N  A  L  C  P
```

Find: 7-word hidden message.

"In the **BEGINNING** was the Word [**SON**]...and the **WORD** was God. He was <u>**WITH GOD**</u> in the beginning...For **GOD** so **LOVED** the **WORLD** that he **GAVE** his one and only Son, that **WHOEVER BELIEVES** in **HIM** <u>**SHALL NOT**</u> PERISH but **HAVE ETERNAL LIFE**."

—John 1:1-2; 3:16

Word Search No. 19

1 John 3–5

```
I  E  M  O  C  R  E  V  O  R  E  E
E  S  L  A  F  N  A  L  A  L  C  V
Y  O  U  R  D  W  A  E  Y  B  I  E
S  A  C  K  E  N  F  O  E  L  F  R
W  R  L  E  H  D  G  L  E  A  I  Y
H  I  O  M  S  A  I  N  D  I  R  T
H  E  W  I  I  E  I  L  W  D  C  H
L  M  A  D  V  K  E  O  Y  O  A  I
U  L  O  E  A  A  N  R  L  P  S  N
A  L  O  T  L  K  S  H  S  I  S  G
S  T  R  V  I  C  T  O  R  Y  F  A
B  O  R  N  E  I  G  H  T  H  L  E
```

Hint: Words are horizontal, vertical, and diagonal.
Find: 13-word hidden message.

3:1   "the Father has _____ on us...the world does not
        _____ us"

3:9   "he has been _____ of God"

3:11 "We should _____ one another"

3:16 "Jesus Christ _____ down his life"

3:20 "he knows _____"

3:23 "his command: to _____"

4:1   "many _____ prophets"

4:4   "You...have _____ them"

4:10 "as an atoning _____"

4:14 "the _____ of the world"

4:18 "There is no _____ in love"

5:4   "This is the _____"

5:12 "He who has the Son has _____"

5:21 "keep yourselves from _____"

Bible Questions

Try to answer these questions from memory. If in doubt, search the Scriptures.

1. What was Jesus' mother's name? _____

2. What was Jesus' earthly father's name? _____

3. What did Jesus make during His first recorded miracle? _____

4. What did He make it from (above question)? _____

5. How many crosses are mentioned when Jesus was crucified? _____

6. Jesus was on the center cross. True? or False? _____

7. A man named Saul became known as (first name only. Also, he was an apostle.) _____

8. Who wrote the book of Acts? (the man's name) _____

9. What is the name of the book that is second to the last in the Bible? _____

10. Which disciple was a medical doctor? _____

11. What is the name of the eighth book of the Old Testament? _____

12. Who walked on water (other than Jesus)? _____

Word Search No. 20

Bible Questions

```
C Y H P Q D F B L D T K T E
R N T Z X R V R V H T K D B
Y R K G M T P M R E N U R T
D Y U L U K E E Z K J V K J
J Q W T R S E M H U C T C F
T D A P H R X V N L C H L K
C K T E H A H Q H Q J T N Y
J R E T H M X G M W Y G R W
J N R E D B T H D N I A M P
L D P R J C L T J V M N C X
N U J O S E P H K K Y V E P
M M A Y R Q B W F V F L P H
M P H P D E U R T F X P T L
N D T R K Y Y L C L X B M Z
```

Hint: Words are horizontal, vertical, and diagonal.

Word Search No. 21

More Titles of Christ

```
E  T  A  G  L  D  C  H  I  E  F  S  H  E  P  H  E  R  D  L  L
S  E  L  I  T  N  E  G  E  H  T  R  O  F  T  H  G  I  L  I  K
T  H  K  I  N  G  O  F  H  E  A  V  E  N  P  X  B  H  Q  G  I
L  R  R  O  T  A  I  D  E  M  L  L  H  M  R  H  B  T  R  H  N
K  I  N  G  O  F  K  I  N  G  S  V  V  D  W  K  D  R  M  T  G
N  Z  V  W  Z  D  A  E  R  B  G  N  I  V  I  L  R  A  S  O  O
B  L  I  G  H  T  O  F  T  H  E  W  O  R  L  D  O  E  Y  F  F
P  M  R  L  Q  P  R  D  M  F  M  B  R  K  V  V  L  E  E  I  T
G  S  W  N  L  E  A  R  S  I  F  O  G  N  I  K  N  H  L  S  H
O  W  T  K  T  V  V  E  K  T  Y  R  X  Y  N  C  G  T  L  R  E
O  E  C  M  P  L  C  H  I  Z  K  G  J  K  G  H  I  L  A  A  A
D  J  M  A  X  Y  Q  P  N  R  G  V  P  F  Z  R  E  L  V  E  G
S  E  H  N  X  R  X  E  G  L  A  M  B  T  N  I  R  A  E  L  E
H  H  N  N  R  F  C  H  O  R  L  Z  J  J  J  S  E  F  H  Z  S
E  T  Q  A  H  R  M  S  F  N  I  C  W  F  C  T  V  O  T  G  R
P  F  Z  S  Q  M  J  T  G  N  G  H  M  Q  P  J  O  E  F  Y  X
H  O  K  O  P  M  N  A  L  D  H  N  Q  X  R  E  S  G  O  F  Y
E  G  R  H  M  Z  V  E  O  V  T  M  G  V  K  S  G  D  Y  D  X
R  N  J  W  I  A  M  R  R  M  F  D  F  X  V  U  N  U  L  G  B
D  I  K  J  K  R  D  G  Y  V  C  T  J  R  F  S  I  J  I  R  Y
H  K  D  O  G  F  O  B  M  A  L  D  T  D  N  M  K  L  L  J  Y
```

Chief Shepherd	King of glory	light for the Gentiles
Christ Jesus	King of heaven	Light of Israel
gate	King of Israel	light of the world
good shepherd	King of kings	lily of the valleys
great Shepherd	King of the ages	living bread
Hosanna	King of the Jews	mediator
I AM	Lamb	Sovereign Lord
Judge of all the earth	Lamb of God	
King	Light	

Word Search No. 22

More Scrambled Scriptures

```
Y  S  E  T  S  A  I  S  E  L  C  C  E  K  R
S  U  S  B  V  M  H  L  C  S  E  G  D  U  J
E  C  N  R  M  V  H  A  B  A  K  K  U  K  Y
M  I  A  G  K  M  H  A  I  R  A  H  C  E  Z
A  T  I  K  R  I  H  F  D  S  S  D  L  N  K
J  I  S  M  T  C  Q  D  A  N  I  E  L  H  H
M  V  E  T  P  A  R  N  M  A  S  U  W  N  A
R  E  H  L  T  H  W  N  J  I  E  T  N  R  G
O  L  P  N  A  R  Z  E  O  S  N  E  O  E  G
M  R  E  M  A  R  K  V  H  S  E  R  M  Z  A
A  D  T  W  Y  T  J  N  N  O  G  O  E  E  I
N  R  M  E  S  T  H  E  R  L  D  N  L  K  W
S  H  A  I  D  A  B  O  K  O  W  O  I  I  N
W  L  Q  P  S  A  L  M  S  C  Q  M  H  E  Q
Q  J  O  E  L  H  A  I  A  S  I  Y  P  L  X
```

Can you find 24 books of the Bible in this Word Search?

Please write the names of the books below.

Word Search No. 23

Genealogy of Jesus

```
R  M  J  V  G  F  M  Q  C  J  L  E  B  A  B  B  U  R  E  Z
A  P  W  F  D  B  R  N  G  A  M  A  H  J  M  K  O  D  A  Z
M  T  D  X  U  O  D  O  K  C  M  Z  M  A  R  O  H  E  J  M
R  P  F  V  I  C  D  H  Z  O  R  A  D  A  V  I  D  M  R  J
W  Z  D  Z  B  A  J  S  N  B  N  R  Q  M  Z  H  B  L  M  E
H  M  R  A  A  J  R  H  J  E  C  O  N  I  A  H  W  M  B  H
J  P  M  H  Y  V  V  Y  A  G  I  S  A  A  C  N  O  M  A  E  O
L  R  D  A  K  P  R  N  M  M  N  H  E  Z  R  O  N  K  L  S
K  Q  V  B  A  D  A  N  I  M  M  A  S  A  S  A  K  Y  E  H
T  R  Q  Y  M  M  M  X  H  H  Z  V  S  G  Z  J  W  M  A  A
F  K  M  S  A  R  &  S  A  H  K  L  E  K  L  R  Z  D  Z  P
B  B  J  O  N  H  H  H  I  R  T  B  J  Z  J  T  R  F  A  H
V  O  R  L  A  A  P  E  S  Z  E  L  I  A  K  I  M  X  R  A
F  A  M  O  S  J  E  A  O  E  W  Y  H  A  D  U  J  Q  W  T
X  Z  A  M  S  I  S  L  J  R  W  J  W  X  X  L  K  Z  R  F
V  &  H  O  E  B  O  T  M  E  K  N  A  H  T  T  A  M  Z  D
B  R  A  N  H  A  J  I  H  P  K  E  L  I  U  D  L  X  M  D
G  U  R  T  N  M  P  E  L  J  M  A  O  B  O  H  E  R  I  K
K  T  B  D  E  B  O  L  S  A  L  M  O  N  T  R  L  T  K  Y
N  H  A  K  D  D  F  Z  X  T  H  E  Z  E  K  I  A  H  A  V
```

Abraham	Boaz & Ruth	Ahaz	Eliakim
Isaac	Obed	Hezekiah	Azar
Jacob	Jesse	Manasseh	Zadok
Judah	David	Amon	Akim
Perez	Solomon	Josiah	Eliud
Hezron	Rehoboam	Jeconiah	Eleazar
Ram	Abijah	Shealtiel	Matthan
Amminadab	Asa	Zerubbabel	Jacob
Nahshon	Jehoshaphat	Abiud	Joseph & Mary
Salmon	Jehoram		

From Matthew 1:1-16 •

2

Creation and Battle History

Word Search No. 24

Battle Preparation

```
S  E  N  O  T  S  G  N  I  L  S  R  T  T  S  T  L  Y
D  O  G  F  O  D  R  O  W  F  P  H  Y  S  R  W  L  K
H  C  D  T  T  E  E  L  F  Y  I  G  G  R  E  O  M  T
S  R  E  D  N  A  M  M  O  C  H  H  O  E  I  B  S  M
K  V  J  P  A  R  T  G  C  S  S  E  F  E  D  K  I  E
H  K  B  N  X  S  Y  R  O  E  M  L  F  T  L  Y  E  Q
L  L  F  M  J  E  N  N  A  H  K  M  I  O  O  R  G  U
L  A  N  C  E  S  S  E  T  C  A  E  C  I  S  R  E  I
W  R  Q  T  W  R  D  M  S  R  R  T  E  R  T  K  R  P
A  G  N  R  P  O  E  E  O  O  M  S  R  A  O  L  A  M
G  E  Y  O  L  H  E  S  F  T  Y  G  S  H  O  Q  M  E
O  S  L  O  D  R  T  R  A  G  P  K  Z  C  F  D  P  N
N  T  W  P  Z  A  S  O  R  N  K  S  P  E  A  R  S  T
S  O  Q  S  Q  W  F  H  M  I  W  E  A  P  O  N  S  M
S  N  I  L  E  V  A  J  O  M  C  A  P  T  A  I  N  S
V  E  L  D  A  R  T  Y  R  A  W  A  R  C  L  U  B  S
T  S  T  E  A  M  S  R  N  L  H  O  R  S  E  S  R  N
G  D  S  W  O  R  R  A  D  F  R  Y  T  X  V  F  M  N
```

army	equipment	lance	trap
arrows	flaming torches	large stones	troops
bow	fleet	officers	wagons
captains	foot soldiers	ships	war clubs
charioteers	helmets	siege ramp	war horses
coats of armor	horsemen	sling stones	weapons
commanders	horses	spears	Word of God
dart	javelins	steeds	
		teams	

Creation (Part 1)

Genesis 1:1-11

1:1 "In the beginning _____ created the heavens and the _____."

1:2 "Now the earth was _____ and empty, _____ was over the surface of the deep, and the Spirit of God was _____ over the waters."

1:3 "And God said, 'Let there be _____,' and there was light."

1:4 "God saw that the light was good, and he _____ the light from the darkness."

1:5 "God called the light '_____' and the darkness he called 'night.' And there was _____, and there was _____—the first day."

1:6 "And God said, 'Let there be an _____ between the waters to _____ water from water.' "

1:7 "So God made the expanse and separated the water under the expanse from the _____ above it. And it was so."

1:8 "God called the expanse '_____.' And there was evening, and there was morning—the _____ day."

1:9 "And God said, 'Let the water under the sky be _____ to one place, and let dry _____ appear.' And it was so."

1:10 "God called the dry ground '_____,' and the gathered waters he called '_____.' And God saw that it was good."

1:11 "Then God said, 'Let the land _____ vegetation: seed-bearing _____ and trees on the land that bear fruit with seed in it, according to their _____ kinds.' And it was so."

Word Search No. 25

Creation (Part 1)

```
P  H  B  V  W  P  R  L  N  S  E  N  Q  F  Z  Q
Q  T  O  N  V  N  L  T  C  S  U  L  G  Q  P  W
Y  M  D  V  Y  R  D  A  N  T  P  O  N  Z  Z  A
K  L  P  R  E  S  W  A  N  M  R  B  I  W  R  T
T  I  H  D  A  R  P  G  S  T  K  D  N  R  G  E
M  G  X  E  M  X  I  E  N  N  S  N  R  H  A  R
W  H  S  M  E  R  P  N  Y  I  T  A  O  T  T  V
Y  T  S  W  G  A  Y  N  G  S  N  L  M  R  H  K
T  K  D  A  R  K  N  E  S  S  T  E  C  A  E  R
Y  C  P  A  Q  V  Z  E  X  W  D  V  V  E  R  V
C  N  T  M  G  B  L  R  K  R  J  N  G  E  E  Z
Y  E  B  Q  C  M  M  K  G  C  J  F  U  Q  D  N
D  K  F  P  R  L  D  N  O  C  E  S  C  O  V  N
G  R  C  O  N  V  Y  A  D  M  T  R  V  J  R  L
M  O  F  R  P  R  O  D  U  C  E  C  F  M  T  G
M  L  D  Y  N  S  E  P  A  R  A  T  E  R  R  M
```

Hint: Words are horizontal, vertical, and diagonal.

Word Search No. 26

Battle of Jericho (Part 1)

```
T  M  K  X  X  M  M  C  O  M  M  A  N  D  E  D
D  J  G  P  T  S  A  L  B  M  N  W  K  C  R  L
R  T  G  N  T  A  V  W  L  L  M  F  L  N  E  E
A  R  D  N  K  R  N  Q  B  R  Q  D  M  C  A  C
W  R  Z  M  T  M  V  Q  Z  G  F  A  R  S  R  N
R  T  D  E  R  E  V  I  L  E  D  Y  Q  Y  G  A
O  Y  L  N  U  D  M  K  D  M  N  B  K  A  U  V
F  V  V  F  M  G  R  V  E  Y  R  R  Y  D  A  D
Y  T  B  H  P  U  G  T  L  N  J  E  N  X  R  A
R  P  N  G  E  A  W  N  C  L  J  A  Z  I  D  P
C  T  M  C  T  R  R  V  R  K  T  K  M  S  H  M
R  Q  Q  M  S  D  M  V  I  Y  S  P  O  K  E  N
A  R  K  O  F  T  H  E  C  O  V  E  N  A  N  T
W  M  B  S  T  S  E  I  R  P  N  E  V  E  S  K
N  B  N  B  K  W  T  D  G  J  O  S  H  U  A  X
N  S  E  C  I  O  V  F  D  H  L  W  L  M  X  R
```

The LORD explained to **JOSHUA**, "I have **DELIVERED** Jericho into your hands." So Joshua gave the command: "Take up the **ARK OF THE COVENANT** of the LORD and have **SEVEN PRIESTS** carry **TRUMPETS** in front of it." Then he ordered the people, "**ADVANCE**! March around the city."

After Joshua had **SPOKEN**, the seven priests marched **FORWARD**, with the **ARMED GUARD** marching ahead of the priests, who kept blowing the trumpets, and the **REAR GUARD** following the ark of the covenant of the LORD. Joshua **COMMANDED** the people, "Don't give a **WAR CRY**, don't raise your **VOICES**, don't say a word until the day I tell you to shout." So they marched around the city once a day for **SIX DAYS**.

On the seventh day, they got up at **DAYBREAK** and **CIRCLED** the city seven times. Then the priests sounded the trumpet **BLAST** and Joshua commanded the people, "Shout! For the LORD has given you the city!"

From Joshua 6:2-16

Word Search No. 27

Beginning

```
G N I N N I G E B J B W Z Y N
G N I N N I G E B E T N X W R
N Z G N I N N I G E B M B X M
L B E G I N N I N G N E Y R T
J H C X M D N T Y W G Y T B Z
G T B X Y N B E G I N N I N G
N B B E I G G E N F K G G G G
I E E N G L N N G J N C N N L
N G G F R I I I I F I I T Z
N I I Q M N N R N N N N Y P
I N N L G V N N P N N N L P
G N N M X K I X I I I I T J
E I I P Y G G G G N V G G N L
B N N Z E N E E B V G D E E G
X G G B C B B X G V C T B B B
```

Hint: Words are horizontal, vertical, and diagonal.

From the verse below look only for the word "beginning" in the Word Search.

"I am the Alpha and the Omega, the First and the Last, the **BEGINNING** and the End."

—Revelation 22:13

How many times does it appear? _____

Clue: the number of David's men, not including Asahel, that were found missing in 2 Samuel 2:30

Each time you find and circle the word "beginning," make a hash mark (/) at the bottom of this page to help you in your counting.

Rahab and the Spies of Israel (Part 1)

"**JOSHUA** son of Nun **SECRETLY** sent two spies from Shittim. 'Go, look over the land,' he said, 'especially **JERICHO**.' So they went and entered the house of a prostitute named Rahab and stayed there.

"The king of Jericho…sent this **MESSAGE** to Rahab: 'Bring out the men who came to you and **ENTERED** your house, because they have come to **SPY OUT** the whole land.'

"But the **WOMAN** had taken the two men and **HIDDEN** them [under **STALKS** of flax on her roof]. She said, 'Yes, the men came to me, but I did not know where they had come from. At dusk, when it was time to close the **CITY GATE**, the men left. I don't know which way they went. **GO AFTER THEM** quickly. You may catch up with them…So the men set out in **PURSUIT** of the spies…[and] the gate was shut.

"Before the spies **LAY DOWN** for the night…she said to them, 'I know that the LORD has given this land to you and…All who live in this country are **MELTING** in fear because of you. We have heard how the LORD **DRIED UP** the water of the **RED SEA** for you when you came out of **EGYPT**…When we heard of it, our **HEARTS** melted and everyone's **COURAGE** failed because of you, for the LORD your God is God in **HEAVEN ABOVE** and on the **EARTH BELOW**. Now then, please swear to me by the LORD that you will show **KINDNESS** to my family, because I have shown kindness to you. Give me a **SURE SIGN** that you will **SPARE** [our] lives.' "

—Joshua 2:1,3-5,7-13

Word Search No. 28
Rahab and the Spies of Israel (Part 1)

```
C  E  N  T  E  R  E  D  V  C  M  M  L  J  P
T  K  S  Q  G  T  R  E  D  S  E  A  T  E  W
T  Q  S  S  T  A  L  K  S  N  L  B  U  R  N
P  E  E  T  E  J  B  P  M  A  T  R  O  I  Z
Y  V  N  I  T  K  Q  R  N  M  I  C  Y  C  G
G  O  D  U  A  D  N  L  B  O  N  M  P  H  O
E  B  N  S  G  R  J  R  W  W  G  Z  S  O  A
S  A  I  R  Y  I  E  G  A  S  S  E  M  W  F
E  N  K  U  T  E  A  U  H  S  O  J  G  V  T
C  E  M  P  I  D  H  C  O  U  R  A  G  E  E
R  V  Q  H  C  U  H  I  D  D  E  N  J  R  R
E  A  R  L  T  P  S  U  R  E  S  I  G  N  T
T  E  L  W  O  L  E  B  H  T  R  A  E  F  H
L  H  R  T  Z  X  S  T  R  A  E  H  K  T  E
Y  H  L  A  Y  D  O  W  N  E  R  A  P  S  M
```

Creation (Part 2)

Genesis 1:14-22

1:14-15   "And God said, 'Let there be _____ in the expanse of the sky to separate the _____ from the _____, and let them serve as signs to mark _____ and days and _____, and let them be lights in the expanse of the sky to give light on the earth.' And it was so."

1:16   "God made two great lights—the _____ light to _____ the day and the _____ light to govern the night. He also made the _____."

1:17-18   "God set them in the expanse of the sky to give light on the _____, to govern the day and the night, and to separate light from darkness. And God saw that it was _____."

1:19   "And there was _____, and there was morning—the _____ day."

1:20   "And God said, 'Let the _____ teem with living _____, and let _____ fly above the earth _____ the expanse of the sky.'"

1:21   "So God _____ the great creatures of the sea and every _____ and _____ thing with which the water _____, according to their kinds, and every _____ bird _____ to its kind. And God saw that it was good."

1:22   "God blessed them and said, 'Be _____ and increase in _____ and fill the water in the seas, and let the birds _____ on the earth.'"

Word Search No. 29

Creation (Part 2)

```
Y H R F K T N R E V O G Y A Y X R
Z M M Q T S E R U T A E R C K Z D
H V F R N N E M E E V H Z C X W W
H R E B M U N A S S T G N O G K G
E D F R T W Y A S R S Z N R N T M
W V D Y I A E R A O P E E D V E F
K M E N D R Q E G G N A L I S E O
Q R G N C K D H M W T S X N S M U
R E X N I E Z Q V E Q T H G O S R
D B I C T N H L R R P K P Y R Q T
T M X A M W G U R N I G H T C W H
Z Y E G A O K F J D S Y S X A T K
F R R T S F V T D Y T E M D Y Y D
C F E M R X Z I B N H A H Z R J W
V R C H A M N U N L G R R H C I H
B C N K T K M R X G I S G O O D B
B D K L S N W F R X L I V I N G J
```

Hint: Words are horizontal, vertical, and diagonal.

Word Search No. 30

The Way Out

```
T  S  E  I  Z  E  D  Y  O  U  C  A  N
H  I  S  N  I  S  T  H  L  E  V  S  I
C  T  N  O  M  M  O  C  U  O  R  T  Y
T  H  A  I  T  E  H  U  F  A  S  A  B
O  T  V  T  E  X  R  N  H  C  O  N  E
M  U  E  A  T  C  H  D  T  E  W  D  Y
O  O  R  T  L  E  D  E  I  E  V  U  O
E  Y  N  P  O  P  N  R  A  E  B  P  N
U  A  R  M  F  T  E  I  F  A  I  T  D
H  W  R  E  T  J  H  T  K  L  N  N  W
P  K  Z  T  H  L  W  Z  L  N  K  M  D
R  T  P  Z  T  E  M  P  T  E  D  L  J
T  E  L  T  O  N  P  R  O  V  I  D  E
```

Find: 12-word hidden message.

"No **TEMPTATION** has **SEIZED** you **EXCEPT** what is **COMMON** to man. And God is **FAITHFUL**; he will <u>**NOT LET**</u> you be **TEMPTED BEYOND** what you can **BEAR**. But **WHEN** you are tempted, he will also **PROVIDE** a <u>**WAY OUT**</u> so that <u>**YOU CAN STAND UP UNDER IT**</u>."

—1 Corinthians 10:13

Word Search No. 31

Victory

```
C M K W Y R O T C I V W V I C T O R Y
Y R O T C I V P Y R O T C I V M B R L
R V V I C T O R Y Y R O T C I V L T T
O I V I C T O R Y Y R O T C I V Y N Y
T C B V L J O V V R V I C T O R Y R
C T B Q I T I I R M O T F P T M N O
I O C P C C C N Y R O T M B K T Y T
V R R I T T T T L R Y Y C R Y R R C
M Y V O O B O N Y R O Y F I O V O I
T M R R R N C R R O Y R T V T V I T V
Y Y Y Y J V Y Y T Y O V I C V M C C Y
M R F R Y R I C V T Y C I Y I H T I R
Y B O O Y I C C I T V R C C V O V O
M W Q T Y V R I T O C O C M T N R X T
P W C C C K V O R O T T N B O O Y Z C
N I T I L I L Y T C R Z O R R F R K I
V V G V T K V D I C X Y R R Y N T Y V
V I C T O R Y V D W I J Y N Y W T W N
F K K V I C T O R Y J V I C T O R Y H
```

Hint: Words are horizontal, vertical, and diagonal.

From the verse below look only for the word "victory" in the Word Search.

"But thanks be to God! He gives us the **VICTORY** through our Lord Jesus Christ."
                                                    —1 Corinthians 15:57

How many times does it appear? _____
Clue: the number of days Jesus was tempted by Satan in the desert (Mark 1:13)

Each time you find and circle the word "victory," make a hash mark (/) at the bottom of this page to help you in your counting.

More Battle Preparation

Look up the verse in your Bible. Then write the correct word in the blank provided.

1. a coat of   _____   1 Samuel 17:38

2. a bronze   _____   1 Samuel 17:38

3. sword, spear, and   _____   1 Samuel 17:45

4. not by   _____   1 Samuel 17:47

5. and when the   _____   1 Samuel 31:3

6. the Gittite had a   _____   2 Samuel 21:19

7. The Lord's   _____   2 Kings 13:17

8. they hired 32,000   _____   1 Chronicles 19:7

9. armed with   _____   Psalm 78:9

10. The   _____   Proverbs 21:31

11. attack her and her   _____   Isaiah 29:7

12. Prepare your   _____   Jeremiah 46:3

13. The   _____   Jeremiah 50:22

14. you are my war   _____   Jeremiah 51:20

15. with arrows from his   _____   Lamentations 3:13

16. they gallop along like   _____   Joel 2:4

17. put on the armor of   _____   Romans 13:12

18. Again, if the   _____   1 Corinthians 14:8

19. with weapons of   _____   2 Corinthians 6:7

20. belt of   _____   Ephesians 6:14

21. helmet of   _____   Ephesians 6:17

22. sword of the   _____   Ephesians 6:17

23. the good fight of the   _____   1 Timothy 6:12

Word Search No. 32

More Battle Preparation

```
T E P M U R T H B G T N C
C K B N S N L T T I O H R
Q L K O T D E Q R I A H B
F M P D W M L I S R A N J
H H T H L S P E I J B F N
K R G E J S M O I R Y L B
S I H K Q A T P O H T N T
S G F G V S V M N R S L J
E H O R S E R E U R R K R
R T B D C A N T L B N C A
T E T C Y D H L T I P Q E
R O D A A R R O W G N C P
O U C V D V D T B U L C S
F S M A B S R R E V I U Q
N N N L X R K S G C R Z L
F E L R J E C W W R K Y I
W S N Y T H L W J O J N G
T S M F K C Q M P D R Z H
G H X L V R K F L V Z D T
H L M M S A L V A T I O N
```

Hint: Words are horizontal, vertical, and diagonal.

Word Search No. 33

Rahab and the Spies of Israel (Part 2)

```
N M L V H I D E Y L I M A F H B F
P A S S U R E D G U N L E S S T C
R E L E A S E D P C M V B Z P M L
D Y T C I T Y W A L L W N T V T M
K J B D A E H R U O N O N H L Q L
D R O C T E L R A C S K E G X W R
C Y R Q H P F E R R P T P U M I S
M B Z H E F S D E W L X O O Y N W
H D H S Y A E I S J P G R R K D E
Q E O R D I V S P T W K V B W O A
J E A E T L T O A K Q X F M W R
D R T U P H E U N E N R U T E R K
R G H S A F S O S R Q X J Z T M G
T A X R R U R S I T L N R K B C J
P L Q U T L U E B K D X N H R L M
J T F P E L O O L T G N I D N I B
N C G P D Y Y G E R B S T R E E T
```

" 'Our lives for your lives!' the men **ASSURED** her. 'If you don't tell what we are doing, we will **TREAT** you kindly and **FAITHFULLY** when the LORD gives us the land.' So she let them down by a **ROPE** through the window, for the house she lived in was part of the **CITY WALL**. Now she had said to them, 'Go to the hills so the **PURSUERS** will not find you. **HIDE YOURSELVES** there three days until they **RETURN**, and then go on your way.'

"The men said to her, 'This **OATH** you made us **SWEAR** will not be **BINDING** on us unless, when we enter the land, you have tied this **SCARLET CORD** in the **WINDOW** through which you let us down, and **UNLESS** you have **BROUGHT**…all your **FAMILY** into your house. If anyone **GOES OUTSIDE** your house into the **STREET**…we will not be **RESPONSIBLE**. As for anyone who is in the house with you, his blood will be **ON OUR HEAD** if a hand is laid on him. But if you tell what we are doing, we will be **RELEASED** from the oath you made us swear.' '**AGREED**,' she replied. 'Let it be as you say.' So she sent them away and **THEY DEPARTED**. And she tied the scarlet cord in the window."

—Joshua 2:14-21

Word Search No. 34

Battle of Jericho (Part 2)

```
C H A R G E D W D E N R U B
L E A R S I F A T H E R I T
H C D E Y O R T S E D H R I
D E T U O H S S T L Y Y O U
W B I S L L H E R T A R V R
S R S Y E G V C E T I U C E
O O H E C O T N H A O S O V
U T E K R L Y A T C J A L L
N H E N U D S D O T L E L I
D E P O E A V R M E T R A S
E R H D E B R O N Z E T P B
D S A T T L E C T O H I S M
W G N I Y P S C T W O M E N
P E O P L E C A S O U N D P
```

Find: 12-word hidden message.

"When the trumpets **SOUNDED**, the people **SHOUTED**, and at the **SOUND** of the trumpet, when the **PEOPLE** gave a loud shout, the wall **COLLAPSED**; so every man **CHARGED** straight in, and they took the city. They devoted the city to the LORD and **DESTROYED** with the sword every living thing in it—men and women, young and old, **CATTLE**, **SHEEP** and **DONKEYS**.

"Joshua said to the <u>**TWO MEN**</u> who had spied out the land, 'Go into the prostitute's house and bring her out and all who belong to her, in **ACCORDANCE** with your oath to her.' So the young men who had done the **SPYING** went in and brought out Rahab, her **FATHER** and **MOTHER** and **BROTHERS** and all who belonged to her...and put them in a place outside the camp of **ISRAEL**.

"Then they **BURNED** the whole city and everything in it, but they put the **SILVER** and **GOLD** and the articles of **BRONZE** and iron into the **TREASURY** of the LORD's house."

—Joshua 6:20-24

Creation (Part 3)

Genesis 1:24-30

1:24   "And God said, 'Let the land _____ living crea-
       tures according to their _____: _____,
       creatures that move along the ground, and _____
       animals, each according to its kind.' And it was so."

1:25   "God made the wild _____ according to their
       kinds, the livestock according to their kinds, and all the crea-
       tures that move _____ the ground according to
       their kinds. And God saw that it was good."

1:26   "Then God said, 'Let us make _____ in our image, in
       our _____, and let them rule _____ the _____
       of the sea and the birds of the _____, over the livestock,
       over all the earth, and over all the creatures that _____
       along the ground.' "

1:27   "So God created man in his own _____, in the image
       of God he created him; _____ and _____
       he created them."

1:28   "God _____ them and said to them, 'Be fruitful and
       increase in number; _____ the earth and _____
       it. _____ over the fish of the sea and the birds of the
       air and over every living creature that moves on the ground.' "

1:29   "Then God said, 'I give you every seed-_____ plant
       on the _____ of the _____ earth and every _____
       that has fruit with seed in it. They will be yours for _____.' "

1:30   " 'And to all the _____ of the earth and all the
       birds of the air and all the creatures that move on the
       ground— _____ that has the breath of life in
       it—I give every _____ plant for food.' And it was so."

Word Search No. 35

Creation (Part 3)

```
X  B  L  A  I  R  W  Y  R  B  R  U  L  E  P  R
G  E  Z  L  V  Q  R  I  B  X  S  Q  M  V  W  N
I  A  T  H  I  V  E  K  L  D  L  L  T  O  L  Q
M  R  J  Q  D  F  V  R  N  D  C  F  F  R  V  X
A  I  R  T  P  E  O  I  L  Z  D  L  L  A  K  E
G  N  W  B  U  H  K  E  E  R  T  O  L  T  C  N
E  G  S  D  R  V  L  I  V  E  S  T  O  C  K  E
L  F  B  S  N  E  L  A  M  E  F  K  L  F  S  B
K  U  T  E  E  A  P  W  W  M  E  K  C  A  T  B
S  N  E  H  L  N  H  M  A  T  C  W  D  N  S  K
K  R  S  O  G  O  E  L  L  P  U  M  E  I  A  M
G  I  N  M  L  K  E  K  R  M  D  N  S  M  E  H
F  G  R  E  R  N  M  Y  I  K  O  Q  S  A  B  L
Z  P  V  X  N  K  B  Q  H  L  R  F  E  L  T  Z
G  W  P  J  Y  L  Y  N  A  M  P  B  L  S  L  L
H  G  N  I  H  T  Y  R  E  V  E  L  B  V  X  Y
```

Hint: Words are horizontal, vertical, and diagonal.

Word Search No. 36

Spiritual Armor

```
F  A  G  A  I  N  S  T  O  R  R  E
D  Y  T  H  G  I  M  V  E  E  R  Y
N  O  N  E  B  R  U  O  Y  W  O  Y
A  S  R  N  O  F  G  O  D  O  O  L
T  C  V  E  L  R  C  O  T  P  M  L
S  H  E  S  O  T  H  E  A  W  O  A
R  E  L  D  R  L  P  Q  K  H  T  N
R  M  M  K  D  M  F  B  E  N  R  I
T  E  Y  J  T  L  P  Z  W  F  X  F
J  S  G  Y  K  M  A  R  M  O  R  W
P  L  X  H  L  G  S  T  R  O  N  G
V  M  T  L  K  C  C  N  G  V  C  N
```

Find: 8-word hidden message.

"**FINALLY**, be **STRONG** in the **LORD** and in his **MIGHTY POWER**. Put on the full **ARMOR** of God so that you can **TAKE YOUR STAND AGAINST** the devil's **SCHEMES**."

—Ephesians 6:10-11

3

Arts and Crafts

Word Search No. 37

Colors and Patterns of the Bible

```
I  E  L  P  R  U  P  H  A  V  E  S  E  P
T  M  N  O  S  M  I  R  C  G  Y  R  A  A
N  I  N  B  R  E  D  O  W  O  I  D  W  L
E  N  T  H  E  C  L  O  U  L  S  E  O  E
E  B  K  D  W  H  I  T  E  D  C  T  B  S
R  R  C  A  N  D  I  T  W  I  A  T  N  L
G  O  A  L  B  D  A  R  K  E  R  O  I  T
D  W  L  H  E  S  I  G  N  O  L  P  A  F
E  N  B  Y  A  R  G  T  H  E  E  S  R  Y
L  C  O  V  E  N  B  L  U  E  T  A  N  E
P  M  O  T  H  E  R  O  F  P  E  A  R  L
P  T  B  E  T  W  E  E  N  M  E  A  N  L
A  D  T  H  E  D  E  L  K  C  E  P  S  O
D  R  E  V  L  I  S  E  A  R  T  H  M  W
```

Find: 22-word hidden message.

black	gray	scarlet
blue	green	silver
brown	mother-of-pearl	speckled
crimson	pale	spotted
dappled	purple	white
dark	rainbow	yellow
gold	red	

Word Search No. 38

Solomon's Temple: Craftsmen and Materials

```
M A R I H N H S R E T N E P R A C Y T G
H A U L N R T G K M E N O F G E B A L B
V C Y X L Z H C O L I V E W O O D Q C D
Y E R F C U B I T S H B M A R I N O D A
M D N M N Y S S T F A R R S T E K C O S
R A H J C V R W O R K M E N S D R A O B
J R A C E N E B C K M L S Y Y M E Z N K
R S N D D T T P A T A R G J R V N R O K
W O D M A N T S S X R R O T R C O S C L
L F B R R S U L T S U C L W A M T H H A
D L R K P E C E M N H D E R U A S E I B
J E E F L G E V E A G R N X Q S Y K S O
E B A N A A N O T I G T I F J O B E E R
B A D E N W O H A N L F P L Q N N L L E
U N T M K M T S L O C V J O C S F S K R
S O H E S T S L J D W Y T A L E N T S S
I N A R A U N A H I T M M T I M B E R Y
T Z M O K G G L L S S L I A N D L O G K
E M Q F P P X R X L O O T N O R I O N D
N O H A M M E R J P R S R E I R R A C T
```

Adoniram	haul	quarry
Araunah	Hiram	rafts
boards	Huram	shekels
carpenters	Jebusite	shovels
carriers	laborers	Sidonians
cast metal	masons	sockets
cedar planks	men of Gebal	stone
cedars of Lebanon	no chisel	stonecutters
cubits	no hammer	talents
float	no iron tool	timber
foremen	olive wood	wages
gold nails	pine logs	workmen
handbreadth		

Word Search No. 39

Music and Instruments

```
S E R Y L L E T U S S S C
T O M E B E F O T R E H E
N H H E M A N S I M N O W
E T I H T H I T H N I R A
M R S N A P K S G A R N I
U U V N R R E I N I U G A
R M P A R T P N D C O S E
T P H S U O P S X I B G T
S E O L A I H L H S M N I
N T F L P L M S W U A I I
I E T E H M M U M M T R S
I R S B C A N S D A S T O
N S G C Y M B A L S R S T
```

Hint: Words are horizontal, vertical, and diagonal.
Find: 14-word hidden message.

bells	Heman	pipes
cymbals	horn	psalms
flute	instruments	ram's horns
harpists	lyre	strings
harps	musician	tambourines
		trumpeters

Word Search No. 40

Solomon's Temple: Interiors

```
T  S  E  N  O  T  S  S  U  O  I  C  E  R  P  W  F  Z  R
F  O  X  T  S  E  T  A  N  A  R  G  E  M  O  P  K  G  T
H  L  L  W  M  N  P  X  G  N  A  P  S  G  N  I  W  O  H
X  I  T  D  L  K  O  P  E  N  F  L  O  W  E  R  S  U  Y
S  D  D  E  S  I  G  N  S  W  K  R  H  C  Z  H  B  R  K
R  G  T  R  W  N  Y  M  B  Y  V  T  X  K  N  L  T  D  T
O  O  D  U  Z  I  A  F  I  G  U  R  E  S  O  H  W  S  K
I  L  I  T  C  A  R  D  Q  M  D  D  E  N  R  O  D  A  R
R  D  A  P  O  T  N  T  T  R  G  R  M  P  B  N  T  M  N
E  M  L  L  V  R  C  R  I  M  S  O  N  D  D  W  F  K  C
T  J  R  U  E  U  R  X  K  K  F  N  P  Q  E  E  L  F  H
N  R  E  C  R  C  R  L  C  D  Q  R  M  T  H  E  O  I  E
I  X  V  S  E  P  U  R  E  G  O  L  D  F  S  R  R  N  R
E  E  O  F  D  H  K  L  V  T  F  D  V  L  I  T  A  E  U
L  L  K  D  E  C  O  R  A  T  E  D  T  P  L  M  L  L  B
P  P  K  I  N  T  E  R  W  O  V  E  N  T  O  L  W  I  I
M  R  K  J  D  L  O  G  N  E  T  A  E  B  P  A  O  N  M
E  U  Y  N  M  N  I  A  H  C  E  U  L  B  L  P  R  E  B
T  P  L  I  L  Y  B  L  O  S  S  O  M  F  G  N  K  N  N
```

adorned	figures	polished bronze
beaten gold	fine linen	pomegranates
blue	floral work	precious stones
chain	gourds	pure gold
cherubim	interwoven	purple
covered	lily blossom	sculptured
crimson	open flowers	solid gold
curtain	overlaid	temple interiors
decorated	palm tree	wingspan
designs		yarn

Word Search No. 41

Pure White

```
L  E  T  I  H  W  T  H  O  U  G  H  C  B
O  R  E  N  E  A  S  H  A  L  L  T  E  E
O  Y  R  O  T  I  T  O  G  E  T  H  E  R
W  E  A  S  H  N  N  O  S  M  I  R  C  L
L  H  M  A  O  E  E  A  P  N  O  W  S  L
E  T  U  E  U  R  R  E  S  N  I  S  C  A
T  S  U  R  G  A  Y  E  H  T  H  S  A  H
Y  E  A  R  H  T  D  E  L  W  L  A  R  S
O  S  Y  E  H  T  P  M  R  D  R  Y  L  P
U  A  K  L  I  K  E  O  M  B  E  S  E  N
R  K  T  J  M  A  Y  C  R  Q  T  M  T  D
N  B  G  T  K  S  R  E  D  G  M  T  N  R
A  H  V  Z  P  R  M  E  H  T  M  Y  Z  O
S  E  K  I  L  S  N  O  W  K  N  P  C  L
```

Hint: Words do not cross or share letters.

Find: 6-word hidden message.

Please find every word in the verse below.

" 'Come now, let us reason together,' says the Lord. 'Though your sins are like scarlet, they shall be as white as snow; though they are red as crimson, they shall be like wool.' "

—Isaiah 1:18

Word Search No. 42

Crimson

```
W C R I M S O N N N O S M I R C F
M N Y X H Z C O C C H N B V L G M
R O M T B T S R R N O S M I R C K
T S N C G M I I I S V F B F C F Y
N M V T I M M P M M M X H M R Q Z
K I M R S S T I N B S R W W I W Y
L R C O O R R R G N N O C Z M N N
N C N N C C C R I M S O N C S O M
O C R O K R M M N R D Q S M O S J
S R C S T Y I F L O N Q D M N M B
M I R M K M C M N O S C F T I I V
I M I I F F K O S L F M M Y N R P
R S M R B J S M N O S M I R C C C
C O S C Z M I B R Z N F K R W X Q
M N O T I R C R I M S O N D C L D
F V N R C R N T G C C R I M S O N
G K C L D C R I M S O N M L P Y L
```

Hint: Words are horizontal, vertical, and diagonal.

From the verse below look only for the word "crimson" in the Word Search.

"He made the curtain of blue, purple and **CRIMSON** yarn and fine linen, with cherubim worked into it."
—2 Chronicles 3:14

How many times does it appear? _____
Clue: the number of verses in John, chapter 2

Each time you find and circle the word "crimson," make a hash mark (/) at the bottom of this page to help you in your counting.

Word Search No. 43

Solomon's Temple: Service

```
S B U T T D E C O R A T I N G T H O S
E E S A A S R E T R A U Q D N I H S C
L S L R I B F S R E S N E C I C R K E
A E G C S A L R E A N A S B F A S R N
E N V N I U A E L R E R U U T R M O T
S I S I O T N D S E E R R L E D D F E
R R T O T T R F S P N N A M I R I T N
A N S S B E E A E T I N M S A C A A B
L U E S E I S E O S E I H Y T I L E A
U S I I M P K F H D R E T O S S A M S
C I R B L E F I L T S R E F O P M R I
R T P H T E N O K E U B L O O O P D N
I O F A R G G C B O U L L S A T S N S
C D G I S G I O C A T S T O T S T A K
E A N W A W Y S I N S H B E B R A E W
S G B R O N Z E A L T A R A T E N N T
S H R E E N R N T N J W L Y T F D T R
T W E L V E B U L L S G Z W T H S X R
T S L W O B G N I L K N I R P S S L K
```

Hints: Words are horizontal, vertical, and diagonal.
Words do not cross or share letters.
Find: 27-word hidden message.

articles	dishes	pots
baths	furnishings	priests
bronze altar	gatekeepers	sprinkling bowls
burnt offerings	golden altar	tables
censers	hindquarters	ten basins
circular Sea	lampstands	tongs
courtyard	Levites	twelve bulls
decorating	meat forks	wick trimmers

Word Search No. 44

More Music and Instruments

```
S  S  M  U  R  T  S  I  S  I  H  N  G
A  L  N  D  M  A  K  E  S  H  P  M  U
T  S  Y  I  C  I  N  S  R  Y  A  Y  O
R  R  U  R  G  R  O  H  E  M  S  E  A
U  R  E  N  E  N  T  T  G  N  A  O  V
M  T  O  H  G  S  H  E  N  S  L  O  O
P  S  R  S  T  D  Y  Y  I  X  I  H  V
E  R  L  M  D  I  D  Y  S  C  P  Y  G
T  Y  R  J  Y  V  Z  K  E  Z  Y  Q  E
S  F  T  R  U  M  P  E  T  W  L  C  T
Q  R  N  X  G  B  G  Z  K  N  N  K  H
D  A  V  I  D  N  A  X  T  A  H  K  D
H  R  P  J  P  W  R  L  D  H  B  W  M
```

Hint: Words are horizontal, vertical, and diagonal.

Find: 10-word hidden message.

Asaph	sistrums
dance	song
David	songs
hymns	trumpet
Jubal	trumpets
lyres	voice
singers	zither

Word Search No. 46

Following Directions

```
F O R L L Y E K A M A L L V
M H T C S H O W N K N P M C
Y A C C O R D I N G R T G C
O N J T A L E N T C E O R N
U I L Q Q E H T Y T T E D D
N A L P B E B T F J T H E M
L T D Y V B T D K K A T S E
G N N O T L H L M L P D U H
T U A U H H E O K T H A T T
O O Y X E V S G E R U P T N
T M T F O R E Z D W F F N O
H A V R F Y I S K R J N C E
M B S E I R O S S E C C A E
K D D N A T S P M A L R L S
```

Hint: Words do not cross or share letters.

Please find every word in the verses below.

"A talent of pure gold is to be used for the lampstand and all these accessories. See that you make them according to the pattern shown you on the mountain."

—Exodus 25:39-40

Word Search No. 45

Occupations

```
W H A S T A D F A R M E R R E N C Y C O
U D O R S R E K R O W Y A L C E O G H I
R N G E G F A B N A S O R R J M U O A E
E E S I O S L R E T R R E R U S N L R V
K S R R V R E O M T E E H E S T S D I A
A M J R E E R N G E K R C K R F E S O N
M S Z A R V I Z N N R E R R E A L M T G
K R M C N A N E I D O D A O D R O I E E
C E K N O R P W T A W I W W N C R T E L
I N R E R G U O H N N O T D A P S H R I
R G H D S N R R G T O R H E M J N S S S
B I P R B E P K I P R B T R M K L H C T
N S W U M K L E F Y I M Y I O M L Z L F
Y E M B T G E R D Y F E X H C Z F R Z Y
P D F X K F R C N E M Y R T N U O C M K
J U D G E T L L H T I M S K C A L B K X
G A R T I S A N S C A R P E N T E R S V
N N C O M M A N D I N G O F F I C E R M
C K W Z T K D Y B R I C K W O R K E R S
N A M E S R O H S R E D L I U B R M M H
```

Find: 6-word hidden message.

archer	charioteers	engravers
artisans	clay workers	evangelist
attendant	commanders	farmer
blacksmith	commanding officer	fighting men
brickmaker	counselors	goldsmiths
brick workers	countrymen	governors
bronze worker	craftsmen	hired worker
builders	dealer in purple	horseman
burden carriers	designers	iron workers
carpenters	embroiderer	judge

4

Earthly Realm

Word Search No. 47

Animals of the Bible

```
G  E  G  Y  E  K  N  O  D  N  E  S  I  S  T  W
O  T  O  W  E  N  T  Y  O  X  E  N  I  B  E  X
S  O  D  T  S  N  O  O  B  A  B  G  H  X  O  F
Y  E  M  A  N  N  G  A  V  E  N  O  A  S  M  E
E  S  T  O  A  A  L  L  T  H  E  A  L  H  I  V
N  E  S  T  H  O  C  K  T  H  E  T  B  E  I  A
O  R  D  S  T  E  O  R  A  B  B  I  T  E  E  N
C  F  T  H  A  S  E  W  E  A  S  E  L  P  O  T
A  I  R  A  I  R  N  D  M  A  L  L  L  T  R  E
H  E  B  E  V  O  A  S  U  T  S  I  O  F  W  L
T  H  E  F  E  H  I  E  L  L  D  O  T  N  O  O
J  L  T  V  L  R  J  J  E  T  T  N  F  X  C  P
J  T  T  K  Q  A  C  Q  G  A  Z  E  L  L  E  E
G  N  Z  V  N  T  R  A  E  B  H  B  N  P  R  M
J  W  Z  C  A  M  E  L  Y  C  G  I  P  C  R  K
```

Hint: Words do not cross each other or share letters.

Find: 24-word hidden message.

antelope	fox	oxen
baboons	gazelle	pig
bear	goat	rabbit
camel	horse	rat
coney	ibex	roe
cow	leviathan	sheep
dog	lion	weasel
donkey	mule	

Word Search No. 48

Edibles of the Bible

```
C  W  Q  R  E  N  I  W  E  H  M  Q  K  F  O
C  G  A  R  L  I  C  B  L  M  T  M  V  L  L
O  N  I  O  N  S  M  W  P  Q  L  O  G  D  I
T  B  R  E  A  D  L  F  P  X  P  R  R  F  V
N  F  R  L  C  W  K  J  A  T  A  E  M  B  E
D  S  T  R  O  W  F  S  E  T  A  D  V  Y  O
R  A  L  F  H  D  H  N  S  T  T  R  W  L  I
A  L  C  E  S  Q  D  O  J  G  P  M  O  V  L
T  T  A  V  I  F  Q  R  N  C  I  C  M  L  F
S  T  L  R  F  C  Y  U  B  E  U  F  F  E  N
U  B  F  M  K  E  A  E  A  S  Y  L  Z  E  C
M  V  Q  D  L  L  V  K  T  I  O  M  Q  K  L
N  P  G  R  T  I  I  S  E  U  L  Y  T  S  P
N  C  A  L  L  B  N  M  R  S  L  H  X  D  K
C  B  M  O  L  R  P  R  O  V  I  S  I  O  N
```

Hint: Words are horizontal, vertical, and diagonal.

Find: one hidden 9-letter word. All of the letters are together.

apple	flour	mustard
barley	fowl	olive
bread	garlic	olive oil
broth	honey	onions
cakes	leeks	quail
calf	locusts	salt
dates	meat	wheat
figs	milk	wine
fish		

Word Search No. 49

Birds of the Bible

```
E  Y  E  R  P  S  O  J  P  T  N  C  R  W  E  M  V  R
R  C  T  T  K  M  H  W  N  T  R  L  H  R  X  K  N  M
U  W  I  B  P  N  O  L  W  B  W  I  U  M  W  G  Y  S
T  P  K  J  K  R  O  T  S  O  T  T  L  A  E  L  P  D
L  A  K  M  H  Y  P  C  H  E  L  L  H  A  C  A  M  H
U  R  C  R  N  X  O  C  O  U  R  L  G  H  R  X  N  H
V  T  A  G  R  E  W  V  T  V  L  A  R  Q  H  H  F
Q  R  L  G  B  E  L  K  K  T  E  H  O  W  Z  Q  Y  W
R  I  B  R  R  M  C  W  K  C  O  W  M  T  S  P  N  K
L  D  W  C  K  A  D  C  O  R  M  O  R  A  N  T  F  F
W  G  S  V  L  G  R  E  N  T  R  H  N  O  C  L  A  F
O  E  N  B  M  N  C  E  S  H  A  M  C  G  R  D  P  L
L  H  N  R  O  D  D  G  D  E  G  E  G  I  M  L  V  L
F  T  V  E  V  O  X  C  H  K  R  F  R  L  R  L  Q  U
M  X  G  R  W  V  R  P  R  E  I  T  Z  G  L  T  R  G
P  I  K  L  H  E  K  Q  R  Q  R  T  O  H  K  L  S  L
P  G  Y  B  C  R  A  V  E  N  V  O  E  W  K  M  K  O
T  N  H  E  N  V  P  T  Q  R  M  Z  N  Y  L  N  W  R
```

Hint: Words are horizontal, vertical, and diagonal.

black kite	hawk	pigeon
black vulture	hen	raven
cormorant	heron	red kite
desert owl	hoopoe	screech owl
dove	horned owl	sparrow
eagle	osprey	stork
falcon	ostrich	swallow
great owl	owl	vulture
gull	partridge	white owl

Word Search No. 50

Parts of the Body

```
I  H  A  I  R  B  P  S  R  A  D  N  A  H
E  H  I  S  E  R  Y  E  O  U  H  I  P  B
Y  T  T  E  C  E  A  L  U  S  F  E  I  A
E  O  R  M  F  A  E  K  A  R  O  F  U  L
L  O  A  Y  A  S  N  N  D  W  R  O  N  D
E  T  E  R  S  T  F  A  Y  U  E  L  L  Y
M  A  H  D  R  S  E  T  D  M  H  W  F  T
T  E  E  F  E  X  J  C  O  J  E  M  H  X
X  M  W  M  G  F  M  W  B  C  A  N  C  N
B  B  F  W  N  B  A  C  K  P  D  C  X  E
E  Y  A  W  I  Y  L  L  E  B  V  T  D  C
A  K  C  X  F  L  K  W  O  R  B  X  N  K
R  Q  E  E  Y  E  S  K  S  B  M  U  H  T
D  V  W  B  R  E  A  S  T  N  O  S  E  S
```

Hint: Words do not cross or share letters.
Find: 10-word hidden message.

ankles	breast	face	heart
back	breasts	feet	hip
beard	brow	fingers	neck
belly	eye	forehead	noses
body	eyes	hair	thumbs
		hand	tooth

Word Search No. 51

Spices of the Bible

```
L  E  T  C  Y  O  C  A  N  E  U  R  C  O  N
V  F  E  I  R  S  A  C  T  O  I  O  M  N  S
B  R  E  N  A  L  W  A  A  Y  R  U  S  U  F
U  A  L  N  L  O  S  F  G  S  N  F  M  R  A
C  N  E  A  S  E  E  A  S  A  S  A  F  C  O
N  K  E  M  D  W  O  I  B  M  L  I  O  A  T
H  I  S  O  A  L  L  L  T  A  I  R  A  S  S
O  N  T  N  D  R  A  N  C  H  I  N  A  T  Y
O  C  Y  U  M  G  A  A  Y  A  L  K  T  N  O
W  E  H  A  O  W  H  T  N  M  L  O  A  N  S
W  N  E  R  W  C  E  D  Y  V  I  E  R  Y  O
N  S  E  N  Y  A  E  R  D  X  D  L  G  L  T
H  E  V  N  L  R  R  G  U  M  R  E  S  I  N
K  Y  O  T  K  H  J  A  M  X  L  Z  X  K  R
K  N  X  R  V  M  N  C  C  N  I  M  M  U  C
```

Hint: Words are horizontal, vertical, and diagonal.

Find: 20-word hidden message.

aloes	coriander	mint
calamus	cummin	myrrh
cane	dill	nard
caraway	frankincense	onycha
cassia	galbanum	saffron
cinnamon	gum resin	

Word Search No. 52
Myrrh

```
W  M  N  M  F  H  R  R  Y  M  D  D  H
H  Y  T  M  Y  X  M  M  H  M  W  R  H
H  R  F  K  Y  R  Y  R  Y  G  R  R  M
R  R  R  K  K  R  R  R  M  Y  R  Y  H
R  H  T  Y  R  Y  R  H  M  Y  R  R  H
Y  Z  R  H  M  H  H  H  M  R  R  M  F
M  X  H  R  R  Y  M  M  H  Y  R  H  G
H  T  M  H  R  R  Y  M  M  Y  R  R  H
H  R  M  Y  Z  R  R  H  Z  M  H  R  M
R  K  R  Y  R  Q  R  V  R  Y  R  Y  N
R  N  M  Y  R  R  H  Y  D  R  R  M  B
Y  Z  R  L  M  R  H  F  T  R  Y  B  H
M  X  M  Y  R  R  H  J  H  H  M  M  V
```

Hint: Words are horizontal, vertical, and diagonal.

From the verse below look only for the word "myrrh" in the Word Search.

"On coming to the house, they saw the child with his mother Mary, and they bowed down and worshiped him. Then they opened their treasures and presented him with gifts of gold and of incense and of **MYRRH**."

—Matthew 2:11

How many times does it appear? _____

Clue: the number mentioned in 1 Kings 10:10 divided by four

Each time you find and circle the word "myrrh," make a hash mark (/) at the bottom of this page to help you in your counting.

Word Search No. 53

Plants of the Bible

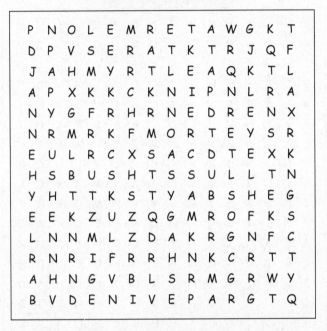

```
P N O L E M R E T A W G K T
D P V S E R A T K T R J Q F
J A H M Y R T L E A Q K T L
A P X K K C K N I P N L R A
N Y G F R H R N E D R E N X
N R M R K F M O R T E Y S R
E U L R C X S A C D T E X K
H S B U S H T S S U L L T N
Y H T T K S T Y A B S H E G
E E K Z U Z Q G M R O F K S
L N N M L Z D A K R G N F C
R N R I F R R H N K C R T T
A H N G V B L S R M G R W Y
B V D E N I V E P A R G T Q
```

Hint: Words are horizontal, vertical, and diagonal.

Find: one extra 10-letter word. All of the letters are together. Look for something you may enjoy eating.

barley   grapevine   papyrus
brambles   grass   reeds
bush   henna   tares
crocus   mustard   thorns
flax   myrtle   vine
grain   nettles

Word Search No. 54

Animals/Creeping Things

```
K  W  N  L  N  V  W  F  D  R  A  Z  I  L  J  N
F  M  A  O  M  R  E  E  D  R  H  G  A  T  S  M
C  M  H  P  G  N  N  M  N  S  T  P  J  R  L  O
B  Q  M  E  B  A  Z  G  O  G  A  L  A  X  D  N
W  R  S  E  S  U  R  W  Q  O  O  M  C  R  G  I
A  X  E  H  V  R  L  D  V  R  G  D  K  K  H  T
L  K  P  S  H  Y  E  L  M  F  D  P  A  L  C  O
L  N  A  S  R  F  P  S  Q  L  V  L  H  O  R
L  V  N  I  J  E  M  F  I  W  I  M  A  K  Q  L
I  B  E  A  S  T  R  T  X  V  W  M  C  B  P  I
Z  H  C  T  K  R  H  P  Q  N  E  E  C  P  W  Z
A  F  A  N  Z  K  M  Y  E  L  G  H  A  O  M  A
R  B  I  U  N  Q  D  A  E  N  N  D  L  D  D  R
D  K  H  O  M  Y  F  O  R  N  T  F  F  H  F  D
S  H  K  M  G  L  N  B  R  N  A  H  H  B  T  D
B  L  L  C  H  E  I  F  E  R  L  S  N  A  K  E
```

Hint: Words are horizontal, vertical, and diagonal.

apes	gecko	serpent
bats	heifer	skink
beast	hyenas	snake
bulls	jackal	sow
calf	lamb	stag
chameleon	lizard	vipers
deer	monitor lizard	wall lizard
dragon	mountain sheep	wild goat
frogs	ram	wolf

Word Search No. 55

More Parts of the Body

```
M  N  O  E  S  E  L  P  M  E  T  T  S  E  H  Y
S  A  S  H  O  U  L  D  E  R  S  W  B  E  G  H
T  E  R  A  S  E  E  N  K  I  E  O  J  S  I  S
O  S  S  R  E  E  N  N  A  N  L  O  C  O  H  E
M  A  G  O  O  R  H  W  I  A  I  S  S  K  T  H
A  E  A  E  N  W  M  S  E  N  R  W  M  D  E  M
C  N  O  M  L  I  O  T  T  Y  N  O  R  D  U  T
H  H  A  S  C  H  U  S  O  O  E  M  A  S  N  T
K  C  E  N  T  T  T  C  E  N  I  B  C  V  E  E
D  W  H  A  H  A  H  T  N  G  G  L  R  E  O  D
H  A  E  R  S  T  P  R  F  O  E  U  T  O  E  P
A  R  O  C  H  E  S  T  O  S  D  H  E  R  W  E
B  A  D  U  S  M  F  O  O  R  T  N  H  O  S  S
T  E  M  W  P  L  H  O  T  L  O  V  E  E  H  I
M  B  M  K  I  A  F  R  L  O  I  N  S  T  W  G
D  J  Y  L  L  P  N  C  N  T  O  E  S  G  Y  Y
```

Hint: Words are horizontal, vertical, and diagonal.

Find: 21-word hidden message.

arms	lips	palm	thigh
breath	lobe	shoulder	throat
chest	loins	sinews	thumb
eyebrows	marrow	socket	toes
foot	mouth	stomach	tongue
joints	muscles	teeth	waist
knees	neck	temples	womb
legs	nose	tendon	

Word Search No. 56

Insects of the Bible

```
G  S  T  C  E  S  N  I  G  N  I  Y  L  F  G
R  O  W  O  R  M  D  S  A  N  W  A  L  T  L
A  L  T  H  H  T  O  M  A  O  T  H  E  E  O
S  H  A  D  M  A  D  E  T  I  A  T  N  K  C
S  D  G  N  A  T  S  I  N  P  T  E  W  C  U
H  A  B  E  E  S  S  V  A  R  E  N  R  I  S
O  Y  G  O  O  D  A  N  D  O  T  R  H  R  T
P  E  D  I  D  Y  T  A  K  C  R  O  E  C  W
P  A  R  E  D  I  P  S  S  S  E  H  V  E  N
E  G  R  A  S  S  H  O  P  P  E  R  M  I  N
R  G  A  N  D  T  H  F  E  R  E  W  A  A  S
S  M  O  R  N  I  N  L  G  T  H  E  G  S  I
X  T  H  D  A  Y  G  E  E  N  E  S  G  I  S
S  E  I  L  F  O  N  A  E  T  H  I  O  R  T
Y  O  N  E  R  Z  Z  L  R  J  P  W  T  G  M
```

Hint: Words do not cross or share letters.

Find: 27-word hidden message.

ant	gnats	maggot
bees	grasshopper	moth
cricket	grasshoppers	scorpion
flea	hornet	spider
flies	katydid	worm
flying insects	locust	

Word Search No. 57

Trees of the Bible

```
E  R  A  D  E  C  R  H  T  N  I  B  E  R  E  T
R  T  H  E  N  I  T  H  A  L  M  O  N  D  E  T
O  E  R  E  F  E  K  R  S  O  F  T  H  E  F  S
M  O  N  E  R  E  A  R  S  M  L  A  P  T  P  S
A  W  H  I  I  L  L  O  A  R  L  S  I  B  O  E
C  T  N  G  P  T  L  H  E  B  G  E  Y  R  M  R
Y  W  I  O  L  I  L  B  R  S  I  I  N  A  E  P
S  M  P  G  V  F  M  O  E  R  F  O  R  N  G  Y
N  J  Y  E  O  I  O  A  N  Y  O  B  E  C  R  C
F  O  O  R  T  M  M  K  A  R  A  O  E  H  A  T
H  E  R  L  T  U  O  T  L  R  A  P  T  D  N  F
O  R  H  T  G  L  E  R  P  C  I  O  P  S  A  S
M  E  S  L  I  T  E  E  O  J  C  U  D  L  T  G
E  T  A  H  E  C  E  E  A  R  A  T  H  U  E  G
M  U  L  B  E  R  R  Y  Q  Q  C  T  M  N  Y  G
K  B  T  A  M  A  R  I  S  K  A  P  L  B  M  K
```

Hint: Words are horizontal, vertical, and diagonal.

Find: 23-word hidden message.

acacia	cedar	olive	stump
algum	citron	palm	sycamore
almond	cypress	pine	tamarisk
apple	fig	plane	terebinth
bark	mulberry	pomegranate	the fir
branch	myrtle	poplar	timber
broom	oak tree	roots	

Word Search No. 58

Locusts and Wild Honey

```
Y  X  T  H  S  J  G  L  B  N  A
E  N  F  A  I  P  B  K  E  Q  N
N  R  E  I  H  R  R  L  L  T  D
O  K  T  R  W  O  R  E  T  M  C
H  B  A  H  T  I  W  P  Y  Y  L
A  W  W  A  I  S  T  E  H  N  O
C  A  M  E  L  S  Y  T  L  H  T
L  W  L  E  A  T  H  E  R  O  H
A  D  L  I  W  E  D  A  M  J  I
N  D  N  U  O  R  A  K  D  F  N
D  P  L  O  C  U  S  T  S  O  G
```

Hints: Please find every word in the verse below.
Words do not cross or share letters.

"John wore clothing made of camel's hair, with a leather belt around his waist, and he ate locusts and wild honey."

—Mark 1:6

Word Search No. 59

More Edibles

```
M Y F P I S T A C H I O N U T S O
O D S A I E D J S R E B M U C U C
E S U S S C I S T T O G R A P E S
D O T E I S H C A B E W W I M L L
O F E L P H I N R R M W A E H O S
E H R I N T A M E E A N A T D T L
C A C C U R D S O A A T F I E N E
G E I S G H M H I D S M W O R R N
S K L E H I V E G E T A B L E S T
M N M P L N H F R K S A P P V S I
R O W L X Q P D K M N F E T B N L
P A E B K K N N J M I R C H Z O S
T T G Y E B M A L P S U Z R W L D
A Z B E M A J L M B I I Z B X E N
O T Y A N D N Z B V A T G Q M M K
G W V S T I B S C K R X T L E P S
J M Z T Z L V L A L M O N D S N Q
```

Hint: Words are horizontal, vertical, and diagonal.

Find: 19-word hidden message.

almonds	goat	raisins
beans	grapes	spelt
bread	lamb	spices
cheese	lentils	vegetables
cream	meat	vinegar
cucumbers	melons	water
curds	millet	wheat
fruit	pistachio nuts	yeast
garlic	pomegranate	

Word Search No. 60

Natural Phenomena: Earth

```
Y  K  C  O  R  X  M  N  J  N  T  L  V  D  R  R  N
M  M  B  E  A  R  T  H  Q  U  A  K  E  L  W  L  S
F  I  W  S  T  S  E  R  O  F  H  H  B  O  N  R  E
I  R  T  P  L  M  A  R  S  H  E  S  H  G  V  R  A
E  E  R  D  A  S  P  M  A  W  S  K  I  V  W  S  S
L  N  E  N  S  K  J  W  X  F  T  W  L  K  T  L  H
D  F  S  A  J  S  A  N  D  T  L  T  L  K  B  O  O
X  C  E  L  L  R  G  R  O  U  N  D  S  H  N  O  R
W  N  D  V  S  S  E  N  R  E  D  L  I  W  K  P  E
A  M  V  L  K  T  G  S  N  I  A  T  N  U  O  M  R
S  S  J  S  D  Y  G  T  L  R  E  V  L  I  S  Y  L
T  G  G  T  U  R  P  M  Q  S  N  I  A  L  P  R  H
E  N  D  R  M  I  I  B  M  D  T  D  S  T  O  N  E
L  I  K  E  N  V  T  L  Z  R  I  F  T  S  N  P  G
A  R  V  A  N  E  C  V  A  L  L  E  Y  S  L  R  G
N  P  N  M  G  R  H  J  O  C  E  A  N  S  Y  A  J
D  S  N  S  V  F  G  Y  F  W  J  E  K  A  L  T  T
```

desert	land	pools	springs
earthquake	marshes	rifts	stone
field	mire	river	streams
forests	mountains	rock	swamps
gold	mud	salt	tar
ground	oceans	sand	valleys
hills	pitch	seashore	wasteland
lake	plains	silver	wilderness

Word Search No. 61

Precious Stones

```
F  D  I  R  S  T  P  E  S  A  R  D  O  N  Y  X  T
T  E  L  R  B  E  R  Y  L  C  S  T  W  O  F  I  V
E  S  Y  A  O  U  R  S  H  E  A  E  L  V  E  S  A
L  S  Y  O  R  A  S  A  L  I  P  T  V  I  N  G  S
T  O  N  H  E  E  L  S  A  R  P  I  E  B  E  I  N
G  B  U  I  T  C  M  L  T  U  H  L  P  A  S  P  Z
I  R  I  T  E  E  U  E  A  L  I  O  H  O  U  A  C
S  E  A  D  H  O  M  L  Y  P  R  S  R  I  P  E  H
S  T  O  H  C  O  O  A  D  E  E  Y  T  O  O  R
F  N  F  E  X  A  R  J  S  S  J  R  T  P  I  R  Y
Y  B  U  R  Y  I  R  I  A  A  T  H  U  A  L  S  S
A  C  R  I  N  F  O  N  C  S  I  C  C  E  S  A  O
C  C  E  P  O  U  T  I  E  A  P  B  L  E  T  O  P
G  O  D  B  Q  Y  N  J  E  L  S  E  U  S  C  H  R
R  I  S  R  T  T  C  L  G  F  I  N  R  R  J  R  A
P  J  U  H  H  D  E  T  A  G  A  A  L  Q  M  D  S
C  T  L  M  Q  R  N  D  T  Q  R  R  N  L  R  Y  E
```

Hint: Words are horizontal, vertical, and diagonal.

Find: 29-word hidden message. Even the letter "a" may be a word.

1. List nine stones found in Ezekiel 28:13. _____ _____

_____ _____ _____

_____ _____ _____

2. List one stone in Revelation 21:19 not found above. _____

3. List five stones in Revelation 21:20 not found above. _____

_____ _____ _____ _____

4. List one stone in Exodus 28:19 not found above. _____

Word Search No. 62

Mountains of the Bible

```
N  B  H  S  A  A  G  J  G  I  L  B  O  A  Q  P
H  M  T  Y  F  K  G  J  G  T  J  T  B  M  G  B
T  K  V  Z  A  E  T  B  D  T  H  B  I  D  A  W
L  K  I  L  R  N  H  P  K  Q  E  Z  F  A  B  J
C  O  A  I  O  A  D  M  J  R  A  B  L  R  C  T
N  H  Z  M  W  R  J  F  O  R  H  A  M  P  A  X
P  I  L  R  C  A  E  H  E  M  H  N  B  C  R  P
M  A  S  P  R  P  A  P  H  A  I  R  O  M  M  K
Z  H  R  H  P  M  R  H  P  N  O  M  F  H  E  K
B  E  L  O  E  T  I  M  A  L  J  B  L  I  L  D
K  R  L  T  B  P  M  O  S  I  M  P  E  A  G  A
V  M  G  G  N  A  H  K  L  E  R  J  P  N  P  E
P  O  N  W  P  N  T  E  T  I  I  A  D  I  T  L
T  N  E  P  H  R  O  N  R  D  V  R  M  S  R  I
Y  L  A  B  E  C  L  M  Y  T  Z  E  N  A  L  G
H  O  R  D  Z  E  M  A  R  A  I  M  S  M  S  M
```

Hint: Words are horizontal, vertical, and diagonal.

Baalah	Hermon	Samaria
Carmel	Hor	Seir
Ebal	Horeb	Shepher
Ephron	Jearim	Sinai
Gaash	Moriah	Tabor
Gerizim	Nebo	Zalmon
Gilboa	Olives	Zemaraim
Gilead	Paran	Zion
Halak	Perazim	

Bonus: Which three mountains from the above list are named in the New Testament?

Word Search No. 63

Nature's Joy

```
L  T  R  E  E  S  V  J  R  M  R  I  E  H  T  T
Z  L  N  Q  T  L  S  E  H  T  L  L  M  G  J  S
T  J  J  T  U  O  O  G  V  H  C  A  N  D  X  R
T  S  J  A  L  Y  N  Z  J  N  L  I  W  T  G  U
W  D  C  N  V  L  G  Y  O  U  A  N  N  P  B
R  N  Y  D  T  G  T  Q  H  A  P  J  O  Y  F  K
L  A  N  T  Q  O  N  L  I  N  H  K  W  U  M  G
N  H  Z  K  O  V  I  L  L  D  N  P  K  O  E  B
R  Q  E  D  F  T  T  Z  L  D  L  P  R  Y  Q  D
Y  K  H  E  T  L  L  A  S  E  C  A  E  P  L  L
E  L  T  L  V  E  T  L  M  X  Y  H  N  Q  W  E
R  P  F  Z  G  H  I  N  T  O  V  G  M  X  G  I
O  M  K  L  L  T  K  T  X  L  D  T  Q  M  J  F
F  P  S  N  I  A  T  N  U  O  M  W  I  L  L  K
E  J  K  V  L  L  I  W  Q  P  W  I  L  L  Y  D
B  N  T  J  K  M  L  D  F  O  R  T  H  V  K  N
```

Hint: Words do not cross or share letters.

Please find every word in the verse below.

"You will go out in joy and be led forth in peace; the mountains and hills will burst into song before you, and all the trees of the field will clap their hands."

—Isaiah 55:12

Word Search No. 64

Rivers of the Bible

```
Z  R  T  C  K  T  I  G  R  I  S  D  N
E  P  R  E  Z  H  M  K  Z  N  L  E  K
V  U  B  O  V  M  J  D  N  Z  N  U  W
R  A  P  T  B  O  M  M  N  B  W  P  G
R  M  H  H  R  A  N  X  O  J  H  H  T
L  C  K  D  R  O  H  F  H  L  K  R  X
F  Z  A  V  H  A  X  W  S  C  R  A  P
D  N  P  I  A  C  T  N  I  Y  F  T  N
N  C  G  N  E  X  B  E  P  D  X  E  A
K  I  A  G  G  N  O  H  S  I  K  S  D
W  B  L  D  Y  F  T  M  L  W  K  N  R
A  G  B  E  P  P  H  A  R  P  A  R  O
H  V  X  W  T  V  X  Z  R  T  R  L  J
```

Genesis 2:11   __ __ __ __ __ __

Genesis 2:13   __ __ __ __ __ __

Genesis 2:14   __ __ __ __ __ __ __

Genesis 2:14   __ __ __ __ __ __ __ __ __ __

Genesis 15:18   __ __ __ __ __ __

Joshua 4:7   __ __ __ __ __ __

Judges 4:13   __ __ __ __ __ __ __

2 Kings 5:12   __ __ __ __ __ __

2 Kings 5:12   __ __ __ __ __ __ __ __

2 Kings 17:6   __ __ __ __ __ __

Isaiah 19:7   __ __ __ __ __

Ezekiel 3:15   __ __ __ __ __ __

Mark 1:5   __ __ __ __ __

Revelation 16:12 __ __ __ __ __ __ __ __ __

Word Search No. 65

Lights and Shadows

Hint: Words are horizontal, vertical, and diagonal.

"**EVERY GOOD** and **PERFECT GIFT** is from **ABOVE**, **COMING DOWN** from the **FATHER** of the **HEAVENLY LIGHTS**, who does **NOT CHANGE** like **SHIFTING SHADOWS**."

—James 1:17

Word Search No. 66

Natural Phenomena: From Above

```
A  C  S  R  E  S  Y  C  L  O  U  D  S  O
U  O  U  K  S  S  S  Y  K  S  H  I  N  I
L  N  N  R  N  E  U  G  D  A  Y  F  O  R
I  S  R  A  T  N  N  S  J  L  E  E  S  U
G  T  I  D  H  T  L  N  S  I  V  S  U  N
H  E  S  H  G  H  I  E  M  G  E  G  W  H
T  L  E  C  I  G  G  V  Q  H  N  O  O  M
N  L  R  T  N  I  H  A  N  T  I  Z  L  R
I  A  D  I  H  R  T  E  K  Z  N  L  D  N
N  T  W  P  Z  B  V  H  P  N  G  M  S  R
G  I  S  S  E  N  K  R  A  D  N  H  R  P
W  O  H  W  M  S  H  A  D  O  W  S  A  Z
D  N  C  L  M  O  O  L  G  Y  A  H  T  Z
W  S  Y  H  O  R  I  Z  O  N  D  G  S  X
```

Find: 5-word hidden message.

brightness	gloom	pitch-dark
clouds	heavens	shadows
constellations	horizon	sky
darkness	light	stars
dawn	lightning	sun
day	moon	sunlight
evening	night	sunrise

Word Search No. 67

Jerusalem

```
B K M W W M L M M R Z T K C M P K M
K M E R W E C E N N L R N E M M L E
N H L G Z L L C N W V B L E P E J L
F N A J N A L H Y J M A L P R L E A
B H S C S S J E R U S A L E M A R S
W M U U R U H L M U S T W N Z S U U
R J R G W R J E R U S A L E M U S R
J E E R W E J E R U S A L E M R A E
J E J R N J J E V M J B L L J E L J
E J R P U K J N M E E A R E X J E M
R E F U H S T V R E S L R Y N L M K
U R L K S K A U C U L U A F R H R L
S U T R P A S L R F S A C S Z W R T
A S G B C A L E E A T H S T U L N R
L A V F L Q J E L M F F J U T R C M
E L L E R F G E M R V P R D R K E C
M E M R R V M K M E L A S U R E J J
W M M E L A S U R E J L C M R K J T
```

Hint: Words are horizontal, vertical, and diagonal.

From the verse below look only for the word "Jerusalem" in the Word Search.

"Then they worshiped him and returned to **JERUSALEM** with great joy."
—Luke 24:52

How many times does it appear? _____
Clue: how old Amon was when he became king (2 Chronicles 33:21)

Each time you find and circle the word "Jerusalem," make a hash mark (/) at the bottom of this page to help you in your counting.

Word Search No. 68

Natural Phenomena: Weather

```
W  H  E  M  O  I  S  T  U  R  E  N  F  R  O  S  T
T  A  E  H  N  E  I  C  O  L  D  R  T  H  E  R  S
U  N  S  N  O  R  S  T  A  H  R  A  S  A  C  W  P
S  R  E  W  O  H  S  P  E  A  A  I  R  E  U  I  D
F  O  T  R  M  A  N  Y  D  I  A  N  Y  S  R  N  W
A  N  A  W  D  T  G  T  H  L  E  S  T  O  R  D  E
R  M  G  O  C  E  N  O  N  T  I  N  U  E  E  S  A
D  R  D  N  A  M  I  R  E  D  N  U  H  T  N  T  T
G  R  O  S  I  P  N  N  S  D  G  W  E  F  T  O  H
I  E  O  N  A  E  T  L  R  N  L  Y  G  A  S  R  E
V  T  L  E  U  S  H  P  E  I  D  O  O  L  F  M  R
A  A  F  L  L  T  G  H  K  W  O  P  E  O  F  B  E
I  W  N  G  S  A  I  V  A  E  D  A  C  T  S  T  W
E  N  T  Y  S  E  L  V  E  E  N  T  W  E  N  T  Y
N  S  Q  U  A  L  L  V  R  R  W  L  W  A  V  E  S
T  N  K  P  H  F  C  W  B  V  F  Q  T  Q  V  B  V
N  X  N  K  T  W  R  Z  D  N  I  W  L  R  I  H  W
```

Find: 27-word hidden message.

breakers	lightning	thunder
cold	moisture	water
currents	rain	waves
flood	showers	weather
floodgates	snow	whirlwind
frost	squall	wind
hail	tempest	windstorm
heat		

Word Search No. 69

Provinces

```
C K R G X L C A P P A D O C I A G J
A B U N D A N C E K B C Y S K K M R
B L O O D M A Q L C K M K U M X N G
T D K M R I N J E N M P G T B F M K
Z P W G T N T R C R K M L N K P K E
C B R A H R E H T A F V E O C D B G
F T L M X F G R Y Z M L X P Q E I D
D A R T W N D N S T T A G H T C T E
G T E G U B L T I S X N S K Y N H L
Q G T J K O R A O Y I N M I G E Y W
D R E L N A H P C L F N D Y A I N O
D A P K N F A G K C C I C C D D I N
V C D G F F Y N U R O H T D K E A K
R E E G T J I T P O O R R C W B R E
V R L X R R P E W S R B D I N O K R
S N Z L P G A N E W K H Z I S A Y O
G G M S K C K N N F P K T T N T S F
W D E R E T T A C S J E S U S G L V
```

Hint: Words are horizontal, vertical, and diagonal.

"**PETER**, an **APOSTLE** of **JESUS CHRIST**, To God's **ELECT**, **STRANGERS** in the world, **SCATTERED THROUGHOUT PONTUS**, **GALATIA**, **CAPPADOCIA**, **ASIA** and **BITHYNIA**, who have been **CHOSEN ACCORDING** to the **FOREKNOWLEDGE** of God the **FATHER**, through the **SANCTIFYING** work of the Spirit, for **OBEDIENCE** to Jesus Christ and **SPRINKLING** by his **BLOOD**: **GRACE** and **PEACE** be yours in **ABUNDANCE**."

—1 Peter 1:1-2

Word Search No. 70

Cities and Villages

```
K M B A I G Z L N A I C U E L E S Y T
L B R N P M K N O P R O M E B Z K W M
Q G V A P M S Q L H W E P H E S U S E
N A J C I C A A E R E B W N E V H Z B
B Z E M L O I S K A N N S P R Z T M R
E A R M I R R Y H D N I A N S M N G E
T G U W H I E C S D O Y L M H I I R D
H N S F P N B H A Y D L A U E L N M W
L N A V L T I A H L I G M I B E E W T
E T L Z T H T R X T S W I N A T V T H
H Y E F S U C S A M A D S O M U E Y T
E R M L Y S T R A Q C T Y C Z S H Y E
M E R F N M G S U S R A T I N G Z N R
P B E T H E L M R A E R A S E A C A A
K C A P E R N A U M B A B Y L O N H Z
J E R I C H O M S O H P A P Q J X T A
T L G B N E A P O L I S T R O A S E N
A C I N O L A S S E H T S O D O M B L
R M N H H A R R O M O G A P P O J K Z
```

Ashkelon	Corinth	Lydda	Salamis
Babylon	Damascus	Lystra	Seleucia
Beersheba	Derbe	Miletus	Sidon
Berea	Ephesus	Nain	Sodom
Bethany	Gaza	Nazareth	Sychar
Bethel	Gomorrah	Neapolis	Tarsus
Bethlehem	Iconium	Nineveh	Thessalonica
Caesarea	Jericho	Paphos	Tiberias
Cana	Jerusalem	Philippi	Troas
Capernaum	Joppa	Rome	Tyre

5

The Gift of Salvation

Word Search No. 71

Redemption

```
R E Q X R L L R R V P N Y
E Z L Q P A K E R U V G N
M V M B N N H Q R Q K N J
Q C E R A T Z P N V B I C
T L E R I H O W H N N R R
L T M E Y S S K R D R P R
E R N M E O P I Q E Y S N
M D E A D P N X R M W F L
E Z M M K R N E T E R F R
R P V L N J R M K E P O D
C W N B K J W H N D J M K
Y M H G U O R H T E J P I
H N L Q P M Z R K R L C R
```

Hint: Words are horizontal, vertical, and diagonal.

Please read each verse. Ask, "What is God saying to me?"

1 Peter 1:18	R _ _ _ _ _ _ _ _
Romans 6:22	E _ _ _ _ _ _ _
Colossians 2:13	D _ _ _
1 John 5:1	E _ _ _ _ _ _ _ _
Ephesians 2:4-5	M _ _ _ _
Philippians 2:13	P _ _ _ _ _ _
Romans 3:24	T _ _ _ _ _ _
1 Corinthians 15:52	I _ _ _ _ _ _ _ _ _ _ _
Acts 17:29	O _ _ _ _ _ _ _ _
Romans 8:39	N _ _ _ _ _ _

Word Search No. 72

Joy

```
P  Z  T  H  A  T  T  T  K  F  L  A  A  U  Z  W  R
T  N  X  E  R  W  O  N  P  L  L  S  N  N  V  X  O
L  I  H  M  Y  L  K  S  A  P  M  K  D  T  T  B  F
U  O  Y  A  I  L  J  T  H  E  M  X  M  I  C  G  P
R  U  B  N  N  I  Y  O  U  Q  N  J  C  L  B  F  R
E  O  E  Y  H  W  R  E  C  E  I  V  E  D  U  M  W
V  Y  V  N  M  Q  B  M  L  L  E  T  N  A  O  X  Y
E  J  D  E  K  S  A  K  N  A  M  E  O  Y  Y  Q  M
T  J  K  G  R  U  O  Y  H  A  V  E  T  Y  W  B  Q
A  U  O  P  K  K  L  G  N  O  F  Z  O  C  N  E
H  H  L  L  C  F  X  G  W  I  L  L  L  J  R  V  T
W  A  T  O  M  R  H  I  U  O  Y  A  S  K  Y  M  E
L  N  R  N  T  E  K  V  F  Q  N  Q  Y  M  J  Q  L
L  D  U  G  N  H  W  E  W  I  L  L  K  I  G  Y  P
I  R  T  E  Z  T  L  D  N  I  W  M  M  Y  K  L  M
W  F  H  R  E  A  A  N  Y  T  H  I  N  G  J  W  O
G  Y  K  X  M  F  Q  A  N  Y  T  H  I  N  G  F  C
```

Hint: Words do not cross or share letters.

Please find every word in the verse below.

"In that day you will no longer ask me anything. I tell you the truth, my Father will give you whatever you ask in my name. Until now you have not asked for anything in my name. Ask and you will receive, and your joy will be complete."

—John 16:23-24

Word Search No. 73

Eternal Life

```
Z L M W T X N L W W T B X N V R
M M I R V N D H Z Z M G O S X F
D M T F F V O S E V E I L E B W
Y D N E T E G Q H H T B M S M M
Z D R V V E P P S A E J M O M L
N O R E L Z D I V L T R E M H T
M G R R Y F R L I D R K B Q N H
E G T Y W E A E E L A G P C H R
D Y J O P S V V L N H G W I R O
N N D N K E O Q S R L M M K W U
O T H E S L D N E P N G Q T T G
C K Y P C A N N S F Z L A T O H
D E S E R T V F O Y I P L V N L
L W O R L D W E N F M L M A E R
R K Q K P S E N D B F K M N H N
K W L A N R E T E D C J D Z Z S
```

Hint: Words are horizontal, vertical, and diagonal.

Find: one hidden 9-letter word. The first letter is "S," the last letter is "N." All of the letters are together.

"Just as **MOSES** lifted up the **SNAKE** in the **DESERT**, so the Son of Man must be **LIFTED** up, that **EVERYONE** who **BELIEVES** in him may have **ETERNAL LIFE**. For **GOD** so **LOVED** the **WORLD** that he **GAVE** his one and only **SON**, that **WHOEVER BELIEVES** in him **SHALL** not **PERISH** but have eternal life. For God did **NOT SEND** his Son into the world to **CONDEMN** the world, but to **SAVE** the world **THROUGH HIM**."

—John 3:14-17

Word Search No. 74

New Birth

```
L L F T X E L B A H S I R E P
L G K K V V T M S S E L N U S
E L H D W O R D O F G O D N P
E R K E I T E L L Y O U P E I
S B O R N A G A I N Z G T E R
N N K A J M W T T T G N O B I
A W N L R H M R T R N I F E T
C D G C K S Y U J F I V G V S
N F M E R E F T L Y R I O A E
H M T D P L N H M J U L D H E
K P Q T Y F K I N G D O M U D
K N F T O F L E S H N N V O W
H T R I B S E V I G E K B Y J
J E N O O N T H R O U G H C V
L R W E L B A H S I R E P M I
```

"Jesus **DECLARED**, '**I TELL YOU** the **TRUTH**, **NO ONE** **CAN SEE** the **KINGDOM** **OF GOD** **UNLESS** he is **BORN AGAIN**…**FLESH** gives birth **TO FLESH**, but the **SPIRIT** **GIVES BIRTH** to spirit'…For **YOU HAVE BEEN** born again, not of **PERISHABLE SEED**, but of **IMPERISHABLE**, **THROUGH** the **LIVING** and **ENDURING** **WORD OF GOD**."

—John 3:3,6; 1 Peter 1:23

Word Search No. 75

Member of God's Household

```
F  L  E  S  M  I  H  D  T  B  U  T  M  V  A  N  D
L  Z  K  A  N  D  Y  H  O  U  S  E  H  O  L  D  H
L  E  L  P  O  E  P  F  O  U  N  D  A  T  I  O  N
S  T  E  H  P  O  R  P  P  O  F  F  K  T  P  L  M
N  C  V  G  O  N  W  C  L  O  N  G  E  R  L  W  H
U  O  Y  Z  B  K  W  P  R  R  C  M  F  O  T  L  T
K  C  O  N  S  E  Q  U  E  N  T  L  Y  H  J  H  Z
R  H  K  K  R  D  G  O  D  S  B  T  L  I  U  B  H
J  E  S  U  S  L  S  R  E  N  G  I  E  R  O  F  R
T  C  B  X  A  N  D  A  S  J  K  H  T  I  W  Q  F
N  W  D  C  Z  S  N  E  I  L  A  W  C  H  I  E  F
K  T  G  K  O  N  E  N  O  T  S  R  E  N  R  O  C
C  M  N  S  D  O  G  R  L  K  T  H  E  L  Z  M  F
L  L  C  I  T  I  Z  E  N  S  D  T  S  I  R  H  C
Q  W  H  W  O  L  L  E  F  J  Q  M  W  I  T  H  L
L  R  S  R  E  B  M  E  M  N  E  H  T  K  V  L  K
E  H  T  S  E  L  T  S  O  P  A  C  A  R  E  Q  B
```

Hints: Words are all horizontal.
Words do not cross or share letters.

Please find every word in the verse below.

"Consequently, you are no longer foreigners and aliens, but fellow citizens with God's people and members of God's household, built on the foundation of the apostles and prophets, with Christ Jesus himself as the chief cornerstone."

—Ephesians 2:19-20

Word Search No. 76

Justification

```
K Y B M G L O R D R B
H J F R R R V Y A C D
D G L U N S X I Y G E
M E O C U S S H R L I
B Y V S R E H E W F F
P E E A D F T A R N I
M J L K S N I R J X T
M O M I T O W T M N S
V Y U T E C P F C W U
H R T T W V D A E D J
G Y N W H D E Y O U R
```

Hint: Words are horizontal, vertical, and diagonal.

"That if you **CONFESS** with your mouth, '**JESUS** is **LORD**,' and **BELIEVE** in your **HEART** that God **RAISED** him from the **DEAD**, you will be **SAVED**. For it is **WITH** your heart that **YOU** believe and are **JUSTIFIED**, and it is with **YOUR MOUTH** that you confess and are saved."

—Romans 10:9-10

Word Search No. 77

Heaven

Hint: Words are horizontal, vertical, and diagonal.

From the verse below look only for the word "heaven" in the Word Search.

"At the name of Jesus every knee should bow, in **HEAVEN** and on earth and under the earth."

—Philippians 2:10

How many times does it appear? _____

Clue: Jehoshaphat's age when he became king (1 Kings 22:42)

Each time you find and circle the word "heaven," make a hash mark (/) at the bottom of this page to help you in your counting.

Word Search No. 78

Salvation's Gifts

```
F  P  R  S  H  Z  P  S  D  P  N  W  D  X  R  L
L  J  L  A  T  M  W  A  U  R  E  E  E  P  O  H
K  Q  N  L  I  C  E  B  E  S  D  R  V  T  T  C
M  B  E  V  A  D  O  H  G  L  E  L  I  A  M  R
X  T  W  A  F  R  T  M  E  I  I  J  N  S  E  P
T  S  B  T  V  A  N  I  I  V  V  W  R  Y  H  H
M  I  I  I  F  R  H  T  I  N  R  E  E  M  V  F
S  R  R  O  X  S  L  N  H  E  G  X  N  M  Z  K
P  H  T  N  G  N  G  L  A  K  P  J  T  V  I  T
O  C  H  E  V  B  L  D  W  Q  W  K  X  N  Q  T
I  Q  N  S  L  R  Y  Z  F  P  O  W  E  R  L  C
L  J  R  I  G  R  E  A  T  M  E  R  C  Y  K  P
R  L  E  A  W  R  D  R  K  V  L  M  T  X  T  K
C  J  V  R  N  E  D  E  L  A  E  V  E  R  V  T
Y  P  E  P  G  I  N  H  E  R  I  T  A  N  C  E
M  L  N  T  N  O  I  T  C  E  R  R  U  S  E  R
```

Hint: Words are horizontal, vertical, and diagonal.

"**PRAISE** be to the God and **FATHER** of our Lord Jesus Christ! In his **GREAT MERCY** he has **GIVEN** us **NEW BIRTH** into a **LIVING HOPE** through the **RESURRECTION** of **JESUS CHRIST** from the **DEAD**, and into an **INHERITANCE** that can **NEVER PERISH**, **SPOIL** or **FADE**— kept in **HEAVEN** for you, who through **FAITH** are **SHIELDED** by God's **POWER** until the **COMING** of the **SALVATION** that is **READY** to be **REVEALED** in the last **TIME**."

—1 Peter 1:3-5

Word Search No. 79

Temples Not Built with Hands

```
D K Y D O B V B O U G H T A
Y Z K Y D W R V L C W Q I L
H M F T L R M F W G B K R M
A X H I R P W H O M Y N I I
N L T C O N H D O G P O P G
D D R Y W R O N O H V W S H
S V A B M A L P G C R W Y T
T B E C A U S E W L E T L Y
K R B W K M K X Z O C P O N
V K N E V A E H K R E R H W
L I V E S Z K T G D I I Q O
M L T E M P L E S N V C X T
E V E R Y T H I N G E E G N
S E V L E S R U O Y D Y L W
```

"The God who made the **WORLD** and **EVERYTHING** in it is the **LORD** of **HEAVEN** and **EARTH** and does not live in **TEMPLES** built by **HANDS**."

—Acts 17:24

"Don't you know that you **YOURSELVES** are God's temple and that God's **SPIRIT LIVES** in you?"

—1 Corinthians 3:16

"Do you not **KNOW** that your **BODY** is a temple of the **HOLY** Spirit, who is in you, **WHOM** you have **RECEIVED** from **GOD**? You are not your **OWN**; you were **BOUGHT** at a **PRICE**. Therefore **HONOR** God with your body."

—1 Corinthians 6:19-20

"I did not see a temple in the **CITY**, **BECAUSE** the Lord God **ALMIGHTY** and the **LAMB** are its temple."

—Revelation 21:22

Word Search No. 80

Salvation

```
D  G  G  R  Y  F  V  M  O  G  E
Z  K  N  W  O  N  Z  T  R  N  C
L  V  W  I  F  T  H  G  O  V  N
T  Y  I  T  D  E  T  Y  R  Y  A
H  T  R  C  R  R  N  J  Y  Q  T
T  H  Q  G  T  A  O  N  Z  D  I
R  A  G  J  P  O  Q  C  L  E  R
M  N  N  C  M  L  R  Q  C  V  E
F  K  L  O  V  E  D  Y  K  A  H
M  S  X  N  F  R  G  X  T  S  N
T  T  W  K  Z  T  Q  R  T  C  I
```

Hint: Words are horizontal, vertical, and diagonal.

Please read each verse. Ask yourself, "What is God saying to me?"

Acts 16:30	S	_ _ _ _ _
2 Peter 3:9	A	_ _ _ _ _ _
John 3:16	L	_ _ _ _ _
1 Corinthians 15:57	V	_ _ _ _ _ _ _
Ephesians 1:11	A	_ _ _ _ _ _ _ _ _
2 Corinthians 9:15	T	_ _ _ _ _ _
Ephesians 1:14	I	_ _ _ _ _ _ _ _ _ _ _
Acts 4:12	O	_ _ _ _
2 Corinthians 6:2	N	_ _

Word Search No. 81

Faith

```
C D R O L A E C I F I R C A S S
T A J U S T I F I E D L L Y O U
R A N X I E M O D E E R F T Y O
E N H D P I M B E C S E H A U S
R E H E E E C A R E S C E S P B
O F O V A R Y O U F E N A I R L
F R S A C T P E T E N E R R E O
E F I S E V T E S A S D T S S O
R E V E N N N Z K P U I S U E D
E Y G Z C X E G B P O F Y S N J
H E C A R G M N N R E N R E T N
T R B E L I E V E O T O M J E T
C H R I S T N N J A H C X J D P
F A I T H L O K R C G C X M D H
B B K N Y F T K Z H I T L G J R
D W E L L K A N Y G R K H N H J
```

Find: 15-word hidden message.

"**RIGHTEOUSNESS** from God comes through faith in Jesus Christ to all who **BELIEVE**...God **PRESENTED** him as a **SACRIFICE** of **ATONEMENT**, through faith in his **BLOOD**."   —Romans 3:22,25

"**THEREFORE**, since we have been **JUSTIFIED** through faith, we have **PEACE** with God through our **LORD JESUS CHRIST**."
                                                              —Romans 5:1

"By **GRACE** you have been **SAVED,** through **FAITH**."
                                                              —Ephesians 2:8

"In him and through faith in him we may **APPROACH** God with **FREEDOM** and **CONFIDENCE**."   —Ephesians 3:12

"So that Christ may **DWELL** in your **HEARTS** through faith."
                                                              —Ephesians 3:17

Word Search No. 82

Grace

```
S  A  V  E  D  Q  Q  Y  B  G  T  H  E
T  O  N  K  D  W  O  R  K  S  M  D  R
P  H  T  I  Z  R  F  O  R  R  C  Z  T
Z  L  R  T  H  I  S  Y  F  L  D  N  A
B  F  A  I  T  H  K  X  T  N  O  F  R
O  S  R  T  F  I  G  K  W  F  R  O  M
R  N  G  R  A  C  E  D  O  G  T  N  Z
H  G  U  O  R  H  T  I  S  Q  J  N  P
M  R  Z  S  E  V  L  E  S  R  U  O  Y
T  H  A  T  N  A  C  C  H  A  V  E  Y
H  I  T  D  B  O  A  S  T  W  N  O  T
N  E  E  B  D  C  C  D  S  I  Y  B  M
O  N  E  N  H  W  U  O  Y  O  N  L  Q
```

Hints: Words are all horizontal.
Words do not cross or share letters.

Please find every word in the verse below.

"For it is by grace you have been saved, through faith—and this not from yourselves, it is the gift of God—not by works, so that no one can boast."

—Ephesians 2:8-9

6

God's People

Word Search No. 83

Heroes of Faith

```
N  L  E  U  M  A  S  N  B  M  C  N  W  V
R  E  H  G  N  D  R  Z  O  B  W  T  F  L
A  B  A  R  B  A  R  A  K  A  O  N  K  L
H  A  H  R  Z  V  K  K  V  G  H  C  T  S
A  W  T  L  M  B  F  F  C  T  W  B  A  M
B  X  H  D  B  T  T  D  B  K  K  M  H  J
V  E  P  K  A  M  Z  G  J  Q  S  P  M  S
R  N  E  H  N  V  I  N  M  O  E  A  Q  T
C  O  J  X  L  D  I  N  N  S  H  R  R  E
P  C  G  H  E  Y  E  D  O  A  G  V  M  H
F  H  L  O  A  M  J  J  R  F  N  H  R  P
W  G  N  R  O  R  N  B  C  A  A  S  I  O
T  J  C  W  N  L  A  M  N  R  K  W  Q  R
B  F  M  O  S  E  S  S  X  Q  V  B  T  P
```

Hint: Words are horizontal, vertical, and diagonal.

Abel	Isaac	prophets
Abraham	Jacob	Rahab
Barak	Jephthah	Samson
David	Joseph	Samuel
Enoch	Moses	Sarah
Gideon	Noah	women

From Hebrews 11

Daniel and Friends

Daniel 1:1-12

1:1   Who was the king of Judah?   _____

1:1   Who was the king of Babylon?   _____

1:1   What city was besieged?   _____

1:2   Some of the (what?) from the
      temple of God were carried off?   _____

1:3   Who was the chief of
      Nebuchadnezzar's court officials?   _____

1:6   Name the four young men taken   1) _____
      from Judah to be trained for three
      years to enter the king's service.   2) _____

                                                                  3) _____

                                                                  4) _____

1:7   Give the new names the four   1) _____
      young men were given by the
      court official.   2) _____

                                                                  3) _____

                                                                  4) _____

1:8   What did Daniel resolve not to do?   _____

1:8   What did Daniel ask the chief
      official for?   _____

1:9   The official showed Daniel favor and
      what else?   _____

1:12 How many days did Daniel ask for to
      eat vegetables and drink water?   _____

Word Search No. 84

Daniel and Friends

```
A A B E L T E S H A Z Z A R R E Y
O U S S T A A R T I C L E S D N N
D I N H G F O R M J E S U A S R E
E M S E P M B M E E R S N O M E B
B O Y D A E Y I L O S I V E S H U
Y O M U B H N K I S E H N A C M C
E I P S E J E A S L U S A A G X H
L B A Y D N R I Z Y L T R C M W A
J F T J N K L O C H B D D E H H D
R Q H Y E M D H F R A L L D N A N
L F Y R G G D E Q H K A E T M I E
L E M W O L C J S V S F M D V R Z
Z H A I N A N A H U I N R T T A Z
L J T H R M N T R L B K E Y K Z A
B D T H S H N E E M K L L T K A R
Z L D N R I J N O I S S I M R E P
P R T L V R M P J F T C K Z M J D
```

Hint: Words are horizontal, vertical, and diagonal.

Find: 13-word hidden message.

Word Search No. 85

New Testament Women

```
B P L A U S A P P H I R A T A T H
E S E Y D F R U I T O F T C S H E
M S A R D O P I R I T I S A O L O
V A E C S I H J O Y E P A N H E M
S A R C R I A R E M T N P D P A A
U T I T E O S N O A N C E A Y K R
S A I S H N D L M A A C D C R N Y
S L A U E A A A O I L M S E T S M
I L L S G S R J D A A O O D N E A
C I L A A S O U R F J U L I A G
R C I N N A U D Y I T H F U L N D
A S S N N E I E S I R A M A D S A
N I U A A A S G E A H T I B A T L
N R R T H T E B A Z I L E L E N E
E P D S S A N D S E L F C O N T N
R O L R K X L B H K T T B L F K E
K S Y N T Y C H E A N E H P Y R T
```

Hints: Words are horizontal, vertical, and diagonal.
Words do not cross or share letters.

Find: 17-word hidden message.

Anna

Candace

Claudia

Damaris

Dorcas

Drusilla

Elizabeth

Euodia

Joanna

Julia

Lydia

Martha

Mary

Mary Magdalene

Narcissus

Persis

Priscilla

Rhoda

Salome

Sapphira

Susanna

Syntyche

Tabitha

Tamar

Tryphena

Tryphosa

Word Search No. 86
Prophet

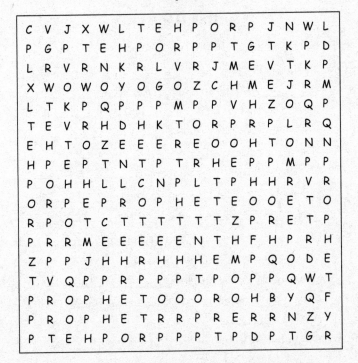

C	V	J	X	W	L	T	E	H	P	O	R	P	J	N	W	L
P	G	P	T	E	H	P	O	R	P	P	T	G	T	K	P	D
L	R	V	R	N	K	R	L	V	R	J	M	E	V	T	K	P
X	W	O	W	O	Y	O	G	O	Z	C	H	M	E	J	R	M
L	T	K	P	Q	P	P	P	M	P	P	V	H	Z	O	Q	P
T	E	V	R	H	D	H	K	T	O	R	P	R	P	L	R	Q
E	H	T	O	Z	E	E	R	E	O	O	H	T	O	N	N	
H	P	E	P	T	N	T	P	T	R	H	E	P	P	M	P	
P	O	H	H	L	L	C	N	P	L	T	P	H	H	R	V	R
O	R	P	E	P	R	O	P	H	E	T	E	O	O	E	T	O
R	P	O	T	C	T	T	T	T	T	Z	P	R	E	T	P	
P	R	R	M	E	E	E	E	N	T	H	F	H	P	R	H	
Z	P	P	J	H	H	R	H	H	E	M	P	Q	O	D	E	
T	V	Q	P	R	P	P	P	T	P	O	P	P	Q	W	T	
P	R	O	P	H	E	T	O	O	O	R	O	H	B	Y	Q	F
P	R	O	P	H	E	T	R	R	P	R	E	R	R	N	Z	Y
P	T	E	H	P	O	R	P	P	P	T	P	D	P	T	G	R

Hint: Words are horizontal, vertical, and diagonal.

From the verse below look only for the word "prophet" in the Word Search.

"The LORD used a **PROPHET** to bring Israel up from Egypt, by a **PROPHET** he cared for him."

—Hosea 12:13

How many times does it appear? _____
Clue: the number of coins mentioned in Matthew 27:9

Each time you find and circle the word "prophet," make a hash mark (/) at the bottom of this page to help you in your counting.

Ruth's Decision

Ruth 1:1-22

1:1   "In the days when the _____ ruled, there was a _____ in the land, and a man from _____ in Judah, together with his _____ and two _____, went to live for a while in the country of _____."

1:2   "The man's name was _____, his wife's name _____, and the names of his two sons were _____ and _____."

1:3-4   Elimelech _____ and the sons married _____ women, "one named _____ and the other _____."

1:5   Later, both sons died also, "and Naomi was left _____ her two sons and her husband."

1:7-8   Naomi decided to go back to _____. "Then Naomi said to her two daughters-in-law, 'Go _____, each of you, to your mother's _____.' "

1:14   The daughters-in-law _____. "Orpah _____ her mother-in-law good-by, but Ruth _____ to her."

1:16   "Ruth _____, 'Don't urge me to leave you or to turn back from you. Where you go I will go, and where you _____ I will stay. Your _____ will be my people and your _____ my God.' "

1:19   "So the two _____ went on until they came to Bethlehem."

1:20   " 'Don't call me Naomi,' she _____ them. 'Call me _____.' "

1:22   "So Naomi _____ from Moab _____ by Ruth the Moabitess, her daughter-in-law, _____ in Bethlehem as the _____ harvest was _____."

Word Search No. 87

Ruth's Decision

```
W L D E S S I K E T L O H O M E V E
E A N D F A I R E P L I E D D E I D
P W O M E N H T H F U G A R A M L N
T E S S N E C A V E R N L E A V E S
Y B A O M O E C U H B U B A C K I T
E N D T G H L C E A M L W I F E A A
T R D S N O E O U D N C B A R L E Y
I D E E I Y M M O U U R N E C K W D
B R N G N I I P T J E T H E M O N O
A T R D N H L A E T A B L M E T O G
O F U U I Y E N O R P A H A T O U R
M H T J G N O I L I K E A H U S R T
L B E L E H R E R Q T F B L O O F M
J T R Z B P T D U T R V L O H N A B
R O N N A O M I T X V L J N T S M N
W L L M X N Y F H R Z N G H I T I R
Z D M E H E L H T E B P K K W Q N D
E L P O E P T C G N I V I R R A E Q
```

Find: 20-word hidden message.

Word Search No. 88
Bible Couples

```
&  H  A  K  E  B  E  R  &  C  A  A  S  I  T  H
X  J  &  Q  B  &  &  Q  C  D  B  Y  Q  R  &  P
C  Z  C  R  K  H  L  &  N  Z  O  X  V  K  H  E
&  &  T  &  B  X  Y  &  E  G  C  L  R  T  &  S
&  T  J  W  F  &  P  T  V  F  A  T  U  &  W  O
Z  Y  &  Z  D  P  L  Z  E  K  J  R  &  &  &  J
T  &  T  L  P  H  V  Q  &  J  &  &  M  X  K  &
Y  N  P  L  Q  N  F  W  M  Z  L  D  D  C  J  Y
&  R  Y  M  J  K  &  &  A  H  E  N  W  F  G  R
T  M  W  W  L  Q  J  O  D  &  H  M  L  V  H  A
V  T  P  &  &  &  B  &  A  &  C  N  N  N  M  M
P  E  L  K  A  N  A  H  &  H  A  N  N  A  H  L
H  A  R  A  S  &  M  A  H  A  R  B  A  &  L  T
&  H  A  L  I  L  E  D  &  N  O  S  M  A  S  &
R  L  A  H  C  I  M  &  D  I  V  A  D  D  C  F
P  R  I  S  C  I  L  L  A  &  A  Q  U  I  L  A
```

Hint: Words are horizontal, vertical, and diagonal.

Abraham & Sarah	Isaac & Rebekah
Adam & Eve	Mary & Joseph
Boaz & Ruth	Priscilla & Aquila
David & Michal	Rachel & Jacob
Elkanah & Hannah	Samson & Delilah

Word Search No. 89

The Kings of Judah

```
S  A  H  M  H  A  I  S  O  J  U  A  L  D  M  A
V  I  E  A  D  H  A  I  L  A  H  T  A  S  I  O
H  L  Z  O  O  M  O  N  X  A  K  F  K  K  K  J
A  W  E  B  A  W  G  V  Z  B  T  X  J  W  A  N
I  P  K  O  J  H  H  I  J  O  T  H  A  M  I  T
K  T  I  H  M  E  A  E  H  Z  F  Z  R  K  O  J
E  H  A  E  N  H  H  Z  S  S  K  P  D  X  H  E
D  P  H  R  H  A  H  O  T  S  A  G  K  G  E  H
E  R  L  S  J  A  A  R  S  R  A  O  Y  M  J  O
Z  L  A  I  I  R  I  M  J  H  B  N  H  Q  D  I
D  O  B  Z  N  R  Z  N  E  K  A  G  A  E  Y  A
J  A  Z  J  R  K  A  G  H  Q  P  P  V  M  J  C
D  U  V  M  R  A  M  Y  O  W  C  V  H  Y  T  H
R  P  W  F  M  Q  A  B  R  W  Q  L  L  A  B  I
T  L  K  O  L  Q  X  B  A  R  T  T  F  K  T  N
K  R  N  M  Q  R  L  Y  M  R  H  D  A  S  A  F
```

Hint: Words are horizontal, vertical, and diagonal.

Abijah	Hezekiah	Jotham
Ahaz	Jehoiachin	Manasseh
Ahaziah	Jehoiakim	Rehoboam
Amaziah	Jehoram	Uzziah
Amon	Jehoshaphat	Zedekiah
Asa	Joash	
Athaliah	Josiah	

Find in the hidden message: Names of 3 kings who ruled before the tribes of Israel were divided into Israel and Judah.

Ruth's Dependence

Ruth 2:1-20

2:1   "Now Naomi had a _____ on her husband's side, from the clan of _____, a man of _____, whose name was _____."

2:2   "Ruth the _____ said to Naomi, 'Let me go to the _____ and pick up the _____ grain behind _____ in whose eyes I find _____.' Naomi said to her, 'Go ahead, my daughter.'"

2:3   "So she went out and began to _____ in the fields behind the _____. As it turned out, she _____ herself working in a field _____ to Boaz, who was from the _____ of Elimelech."

2:4   "Just then Boaz _____ from Bethlehem and _____ the harvesters, 'The _____ be with you!' 'The Lord _____ you!' they called back."

2:5   "Boaz asked the _____ of his harvesters, 'Whose young _____ is that?'"

2:8   "Boaz said to Ruth, 'My _____, listen to me. Don't go and glean in _____ field and don't go away from here. Stay here with my _____ girls.'"

2:15 "As she got up to glean, Boaz gave _____ to his men, 'Even if she gathers among the _____, don't embarrass her.'"

2:16 "'Rather, pull out some _____ for her from the bundles and leave them for her to pick up, and don't _____ her.'"

2:20 "'The Lord bless him!' Naomi said to her daughter-in-law. 'He has not _____ showing his _____ to the living and the dead.' She added, 'That man is our close relative; he is one of our kinsman-_____.'"

Word Search No. 90

Ruth's Dependence

```
F  P  T  S  R  E  T  S  E  V  R  A  H  K  N  T  B
N  Y  D  D  S  P  Y  S  S  R  E  B  U  K  E  N  P
F  F  E  F  T  C  P  E  S  P  S  R  Z  R  F  Q  W
D  K  P  I  A  L  W  L  E  R  R  E  T  W  R  Q  C
N  H  P  E  L  A  N  B  N  G  E  H  N  C  E  Z  A
U  C  O  L  K  N  T  B  D  L  D  T  A  L  D  G  R
O  E  T  D  S  P  P  Q  N  M  R  O  V  G  E  R  R
F  L  S  S  P  N  T  N  I  L  O  N  R  B  E  E  I
R  E  T  H  G  U  A  D  K  Y  N  A  E  N  M  E  V
K  M  E  V  I  T  A  L  E  R  F  M  S  M  E  T  E
K  I  C  D  J  D  P  A  N  Y  O  N  E  T  R  E  D
L  L  F  A  V  O  R  G  N  I  D  N  A  T  S  D  Q
O  E  J  N  N  S  S  E  T  I  B  A  O  M  V  Q  V
R  H  C  H  G  P  B  O  A  Z  J  Z  L  X  C  M  T
D  H  C  G  Y  R  M  G  N  I  G  N  O  L  E  B
L  E  F  T  O  V  E  R  D  N  N  A  M  E  R  O  F
W  O  M  A  N  G  L  E  A  N  S  H  E  A  V  E  S
```

Hint: Words are horizontal, vertical, and diagonal.

Word Search No. 91

The Noble Bereans

```
W  C  C  D  S  E  L  U  A  P  Y  B  T
O  J  H  K  W  E  G  H  E  S  L  H  S
N  H  A  N  C  C  E  A  N  M  E  J  C
Y  X  R  D  A  Y  G  A  S  S  L  K  R
L  E  A  G  V  E  D  S  S  Q  F  I
Q  U  C  T  R  R  E  A  N  N  E  W  P
Y  R  T  N  E  N  L  D  K  O  K  M  T
M  T  E  B  I  O  L  L  D  F  B  G  U
R  S  R  M  N  M  R  T  N  I  T  L  R
S  Z  A  I  F  M  O  R  E  P  A  L  E
N  X  A  N  N  R  Q  L  N  R  E  S  S
E  N  D  E  V  I  E  C  E  R  R  N  L
S  B  R  G  Q  J  N  R  B  R  G  Y  Q
```

Hint: Words are horizontal, vertical, and diagonal.

"**NOW** the **BEREANS** were of **MORE NOBLE CHARACTER** than the **THESSALONIANS**, for they **RECEIVED** the **MESSAGE** with **GREAT EAGERNESS** and **EXAMINED** the **SCRIPTURES** every **DAY** to **SEE** if what **PAUL SAID** was **TRUE**."

—Acts 17:11

Word Search No. 92

Zacchaeus' Determination

```
W  B  N  R  K  Y  A  T  S  T  S  U  M  W  P  Z  N  Q
P  R  E  A  C  H  E  D  Y  B  N  L  G  U  E  S  T  G
T  R  O  H  S  N  S  N  O  I  S  S  E  S  S  O  P  Z
K  M  P  V  B  D  E  B  M  I  L  C  E  N  W  R  Q  N
X  K  D  K  Y  R  G  F  Y  N  P  H  N  X  L  R  T  D
Y  N  G  D  P  E  J  B  H  K  M  P  T  E  S  U  O  H
L  T  T  A  D  T  V  E  T  Y  Q  U  E  K  T  Z  S  W
E  X  A  E  Q  T  D  C  L  D  M  D  R  P  G  A  A  E
T  T  X  H  Y  U  W  A  A  O  N  O  E  E  N  C  L  L
A  L  C  A  L  M  K  U  E  B  K  O  D  O  I  C  V  C
I  O  O  N  D  F  L  S  W  Y  N  T  M  P  M  H  A  O
D  O  L  A  A  V  J  E  C  N  Z  S  K  L  O  A  T  M
E  K  L  R  L  Z  S  Y  C  A  M  O  R  E  C  E  I  E
M  E  E  M  G  M  K  K  G  N  R  H  H  T  X  U  O  D
M  D  C  T  A  N  Y  T  H  I  N  G  A  Z  W  S  N  M
I  U  T  S  E  M  I  T  R  U  O  F  L  B  L  O  O  K
M  P  O  C  D  E  T  N  A  W  F  D  F  M  P  C  R  R
C  M  R  K  P  A  S  S  I  N  G  N  M  C  R  O  W  D
```

"Jesus **ENTERED** Jericho…**PASSING** through…**ZACCHAEUS**…a chief **TAX COLLECTOR**…was **WEALTHY**. He **WANTED** to see who Jesus was, but being a **SHORT** man he could not, **BECAUSE** of the **CROWD**. So he **RAN AHEAD** and **CLIMBED** a **SYCAMORE**-fig tree to see him, since Jesus was **COMING** that way.

"When Jesus **REACHED** the spot, he **LOOKED UP** and said to him, 'Zacchaeus, come down **IMMEDIATELY**. I **MUST STAY** at your house today.' So he came down at once and **WELCOMED** him **GLADLY**.

"All the **PEOPLE** saw this and began to **MUTTER**, 'He has gone to be the **GUEST** of a "sinner." ' But Zacchaeus **STOOD UP** and said to the Lord, '**LOOK**, Lord!…I give **HALF** of my **POSSESSIONS** to the poor, and if I have cheated **ANYBODY** out of **ANYTHING**, I will pay back **FOUR TIMES** the amount.' Jesus said to him, 'Today **SALVATION** has come to this **HOUSE**.'"

—Luke 19:1-9

Paul's Conversion

"Meanwhile, Saul was still **BREATHING** out **MURDEROUS THREATS** against the Lord's disciples. He…asked [the high priest] for letters to the **SYNAGOGUES** in **DAMASCUS**, so that if he found any there who belonged to the Way…he might take them as **PRISONERS** to **JERUSALEM**. As he neared Damascus on his **JOURNEY**, suddenly a **LIGHT** from **HEAVEN** flashed around him. He fell to the ground and **HEARD** a voice say to him, 'Saul, **SAUL**, why do you **PERSECUTE** me?'

" 'Who are you, Lord?' Saul asked.

" 'I am **JESUS**, whom you are persecuting,' he replied.

" 'Now get up and go into the city, and you will be told what you must do.'

"The men **TRAVELING** with Saul stood there **SPEECHLESS**; they heard the **SOUND** but did not see anyone. Saul got up from the **GROUND**, but when he opened his eyes he could see nothing. So they led him by the hand into Damascus. For three days he was **BLIND**, and did not eat or drink anything.

"In Damascus there was a **DISCIPLE** named **ANANIAS**. The Lord called to him in a **VISION**, 'Ananias!'

" 'Yes, Lord,' he answered.

"The Lord told him, 'Go to the house of **JUDAS** on **STRAIGHT** Street and ask for a man from **TARSUS** named Saul, for he is **PRAYING**. In a vision he has seen a man named Ananias come and place his hands on him to **RESTORE** his **SIGHT**.'

" 'Lord,' Ananias answered, 'I have heard many **REPORTS** about this man and all the **HARM** he has done to your saints in Jerusalem. And he has come here with **AUTHORITY** from the chief **PRIESTS** to arrest all who call on your name.'

"But the Lord said to Ananias, 'Go! This man is my **CHOSEN** instrument to carry my name before the **GENTILES** and their kings and before the people of Israel. I will show him how much he must **SUFFER** for my name.'

"Then Ananias went to the **HOUSE** and entered it. Placing his hands on Saul, he said, 'Brother Saul, the Lord—Jesus, who **APPEARED** to you on the **ROAD** as you were coming here—has sent me so that you may see again and be **FILLED** with the Holy Spirit.' **IMMEDIATELY** something like scales fell from Saul's eyes, and he could see again. He got up and was **BAPTIZED**, and after taking some **FOOD**, he **REGAINED** his **STRENGTH**."

—Acts 9:1-19

Word Search No. 93

Paul's Conversion

```
W  X  S  P  E  E  C  H  L  E  S  S  P  B  T  R  H  K
R  G  Z  D  H  F  O  O  D  J  E  R  U  S  A  L  E  M
Z  T  E  T  A  U  T  H  O  R  I  T  Y  N  N  E  T  D
S  K  G  N  I  L  E  V  A  R  T  R  N  N  Z  L  B  B
K  U  P  J  T  S  E  U  G  O  G  A  N  Y  S  P  T  Q
C  P  F  R  E  I  W  V  P  N  E  S  O  H  C  I  H  E
R  N  J  F  I  S  L  K  N  Q  R  D  N  S  P  C  G  T
E  S  W  Z  E  S  U  E  L  B  E  V  T  C  P  S  I  U
G  R  U  N  L  R  O  S  S  L  A  R  I  V  L  I  A  C
A  R  M  O  R  S  J  N  L  H  E  P  M  S  H  D  R  E
I  Z  T  H  R  H  U  I  E  N  G  G  T  A  I  M  T  S
N  L  N  N  B  E  F  C  G  R  N  J  R  I  P  O  S  R
E  T  X  N  S  G  D  T  S  I  S  M  G  B  Z  K  N  E
D  A  O  R  A  J  H  R  Y  A  X  B  Y  L  R  E  P  P
R  N  W  K  I  G  W  A  U  V  M  J  Q  I  E  S  D  B
N  T  L  L  N  T  R  W  K  M  U  A  M  N  P  T  P  G
Q  E  X  C  A  P  J  M  N  D  K  Y  D  D  O  A  L  R
N  S  V  K  N  Z  L  B  A  C  L  G  X  J  R  E  W  O
M  G  U  A  A  M  T  S  G  E  B  Y  J  L  T  R  M  U
Y  L  Q  S  E  M  G  Z  T  R  D  J  E  R  S  H  M  N
F  C  U  Y  R  H  Q  A  E  E  L  K  S  B  F  T  B  D
T  N  X  A  Y  A  I  A  R  R  T  N  U  D  R  A  E  H
H  M  Y  T  S  D  T  A  E  J  J  L  O  X  T  Z  N  X
G  T  R  M  E  H  E  S  D  Z  O  X  H  X  P  T  L  R
I  L  J  M  I  P  T  N  T  B  U  V  J  Q  N  C  C  D
S  C  M  N  P  O  U  M  Y  P  R  M  Y  M  R  T  T  H
J  I  G  A  R  O  C  R  Z  T  N  T  H  G  I  L  D  N
K  J  N  E  S  T  H  M  Z  M  E  V  H  G  C  M  L  T
D  B  P  R  I  E  S  T  S  Y  Y  R  Q  N  M  T  R  H
```

Hint: Words are horizontal, vertical, and diagonal.

Word Search No. 94

Family

```
Y J Y W Y Y F A M I L Y F
L M L K L Y Y A B M L Y A
I J I I I F L L M T L T M
M F M P M F A I I C Z I
A A A H A K F M M M L D L
F M F M F A Y A I A A Y Y
R I I R M L F F M L F F V
N L G I I Z B A M I Y P N
Y Y L M Y L I M A F L V N
K Y A L F A M I L Y N Y G
N F J F A M I L Y W Q X P
F A M I L Y J Y L I M A F
F A M I L Y K Y L I M A F
```

Hint: Words are horizontal, vertical, and diagonal.

From the verse below look only for the word "family" in the Word Search.

"As we have opportunity, let us do good to all people, especially to those who belong to the **FAMILY** of believers."

—Galatians 6:10

How many times does it appear? _____
Clue: the number of elders in Revelation 11:16 who fell on their faces and worshiped God

Each time you find and circle the word "family," make a hash mark (/) at the bottom of this page to help you in your counting.

Word Search No. 95

Timothy

```
O S L A U O Y N I S E V I L J
E P L Y S T R A H S U S L O V
E O S M M Y O U T Y O U R P A
R K E O U N T S I R E H T O M
A E N T I D G R A E A N D P A
R W F H N S E T F B N T S D O
Y E A E O R O I E R U L O V E
J L T R C E E M R E S U S Z C
S L H E I H T O E D B T N J N
S O E U T T J T C N T Q V L Y
E F R N T O W H N H H M C T B
W H M I T R H Y I J K Y Q C L
E I L C X B Z N S K J N H F T
J M B E L I E V E R K E E R G
G R A N D M O T H E R L O I S
```

Find: 11-word hidden message.

"I have been reminded of your **SINCERE FAITH**, which first lived in your **GRANDMOTHER LOIS** and in your **MOTHER EUNICE** and, I am persuaded, now **LIVES IN YOU ALSO**."

—2 Timothy 1:5

"He came to **DERBE** and then to **LYSTRA**, where a disciple named **TIMOTHY** lived, whose **MOTHER** was a **JEWESS** and a **BELIEVER**, but whose **FATHER** was a **GREEK**. The **BROTHERS** at Lystra and **ICONIUM** SPOKE WELL OF HIM."

—Acts 16:1-2

Ruth's Delight

Ruth 3–4:17

3:1-2   "One day Naomi [Ruth's] mother-in-law said to her, 'My daughter, should I not try to find a home for you, where you will be well _____ for?…Tonight [Boaz] will be _____ barley on the threshing floor.' "

3:7-9   "When Boaz had finished _____ and _____ and was in good spirits, he went over to lie down at the far end of the _____ pile. Ruth _____ quietly, _____his feet and lay down. In the _____ of the night something startled the man, and he turned and discovered a _____ lying at his feet. 'Who are you?' he asked. 'I am your servant Ruth,' she said. 'Spread the _____ of your _____ over me, since you are a kinsman-redeemer.' "

3:11   " 'Now, my daughter, don't be afraid. I will do for you all you _____. All my fellow _____ know that you are a woman of noble character.' "

3:18   "Then Naomi said, 'Wait, my daughter, until you find out what _____. For the man will not rest until the _____ is _____ today.' "

4:9   "Then Boaz _____ to the elders and all the people, 'Today you are _____ that I have _____ from Naomi all the _____ of Elimelech, Kilion and Mahlon.' "

4:10   " 'I have also _____ Ruth the Moabitess, Mahlon's _____, as my wife, in order to maintain the name of the dead with his property, so that his name will not _____ from among his family or from the town records. Today you are witnesses!' "

4:13   "So Boaz took Ruth and she _____ his wife. Then he went to her, and the Lord enabled her to _____, and she gave birth to a son."

4:17   "The women living there said, 'Naomi has a son.' And they named him _____. He was the father of Jesse, the _____ of David."

Word Search No. 96

Ruth's Delight

```
M S E S S E N T I W D R T R X F
E B O U G H T H L H E G R A I N
M T K R E T T A M E R E H T A F
A N T R Q E X P T L I Y N F B Y
C E Q U M A R P K D U Z A X K G
E M A N L T L E R D Q V M W W V
B R P C V I F N B I C W O D I W
R A P O P N G S Z M A K W F D Q
A G R V R G R E N R O C Q N E C
E L O E O D R I N K I N G X L O
P M A R P T K R H R R K S A T N
P T C E E A N N O U N C E D T C
A J H D R D E D I V O R P Y E E
S J E K T G N I W O N N I W S I
I N D M Y R R T O W N S M E N V
D K K F T O B E D R F G N L N E
```

Solutions

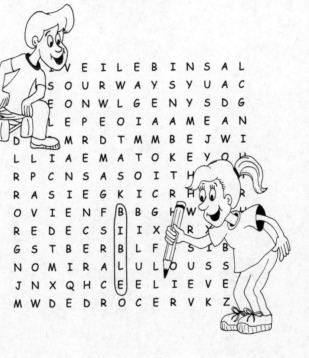

```
I V E I L E B I N S A L
S O U R W A Y S Y U A C
E O N W L G E N Y S D G
L E P E O I A A M E A N
D M R D T M M B E J W I
L L I A E M A T O K E Y O U
R P C N S A S O I T H
R A S I E G K I C R H R
O V I E N F B B G H W
R E D E C S I I X R
G S T B E R B L F S I B
N O M I R A L U L O U S S
J N X Q H C E E L I E V E
M W D E D R O C E R V K Z
```

Word Search No. 1
No Other Savior

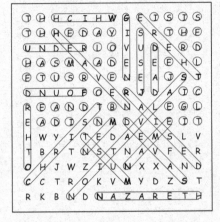

Word Search No. 2
New Testament Books

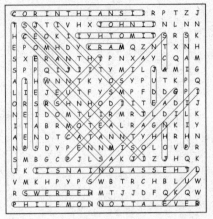

Word Search No. 3
Precious Things in Scripture

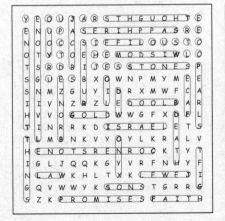

Word Search No. 4
The First Miracle of Jesus

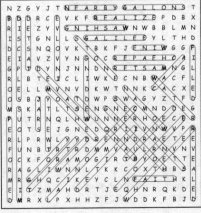

Word Search No. 5
Jesus

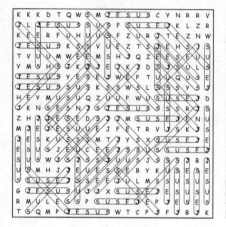

Word Search No. 6
Old Testament Books: History/Poetry

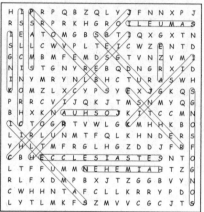

Word Search No. 7
I AM's of Jesus in John 10–20

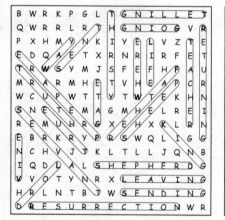

Word Search No. 8
Jesus Heals Bartimaeus

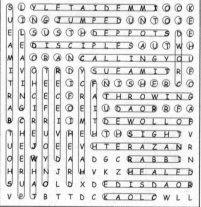

Word Search No. 9
All Scripture

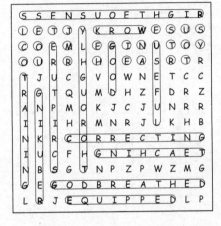

Word Search No. 10
Bible Facts

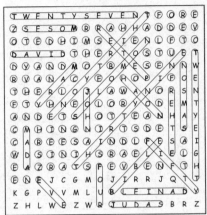

Word Search No. 11
Names and Titles of Christ

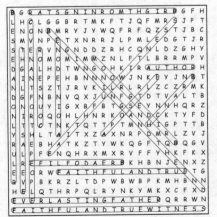

Word Search No. 12
Scrambled Scriptures

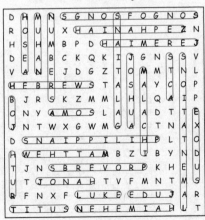

Word Search No. 13

Miraculous Signs

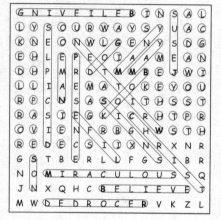

Word Search No. 14

Scripture Challenge

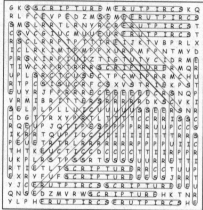

Word Search No. 15

Son of Man

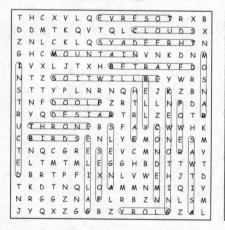

Word Search No. 16

1 John 1–2

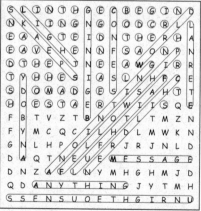

Word Search No. 17

Old Testament Books: Prophets

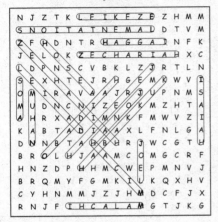

Word Search No. 18

Eternal Son of God

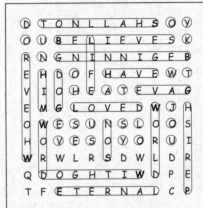

Word Search No. 19

1 John 3–5

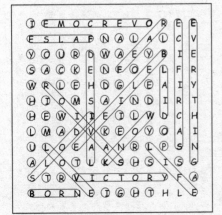

Word Search No. 20

Bible Questions

Word Search No. 21
More Titles of Christ

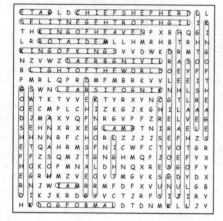

Word Search No. 22
More Scrambled Scriptures

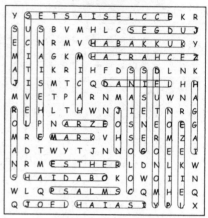

Word Search No. 23
Genealogy of Jesus

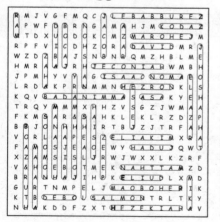

Word Search No. 24
Battle Preparation

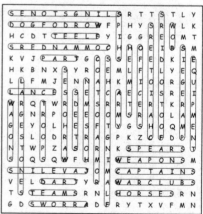

Word Search No. 25
Creation (Part 1)

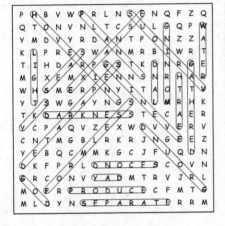

Word Search No. 26
Battle of Jericho (Part 1)

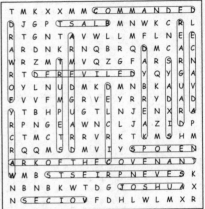

Word Search No. 27
Beginning

Word Search No. 28
Rehab and the Spies of Israel (Part 1)

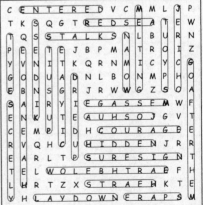

Word Search No. 29

Creation (Part 2)

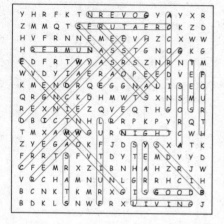

Word Search No. 30

The Way Out

Word Search No. 31

Victory

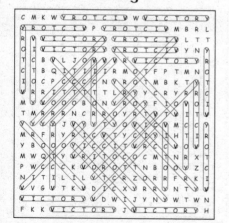

Word Search No. 32

More Battle Preparation

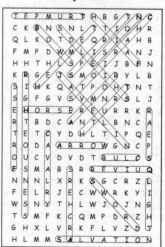

Word Search No. 33
Rehab and the Spies of Israel (Part 2)

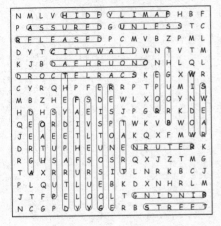

Word Search No. 34
Battle of Jericho (Part 2)

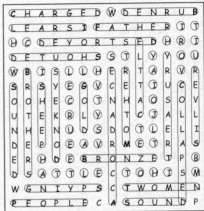

Word Search No. 35
Creation (Part 3)

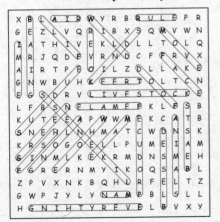

Word Search No. 36
Spiritual Armor

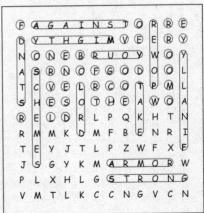

Word Search No. 37

Colors and Patterns of the Bible

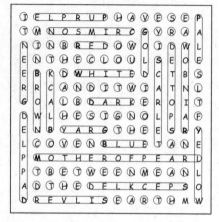

Word Search No. 38

Solomon's Temple: Craftsmen and Materials

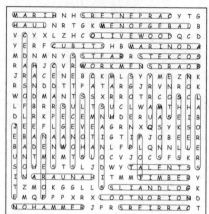

Word Search No. 39

Music and Instruments

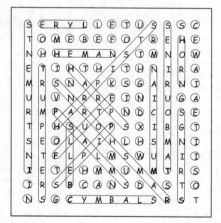

Word Search No. 40

Solomon's Temple: Interiors

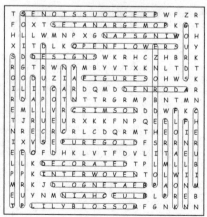

Word Search No. 41

Pure White

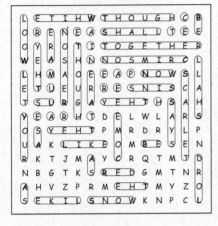

Word Search No. 42

Crimson

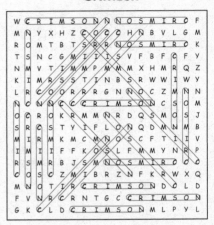

Word Search No. 43

Solomon's Temple: Service

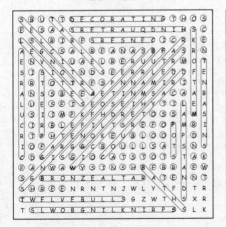

Word Search No. 44

More Music and Instruments

Word Search No. 45

Occupations

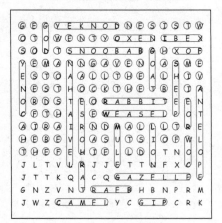

Word Search No. 46

Following Directions

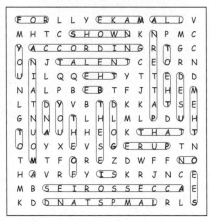

Word Search No. 47

Animals of the Bible

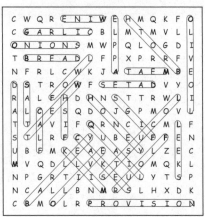

Word Search No. 48

Edibles of the Bible

Word Search No. 49
Birds of the Bible

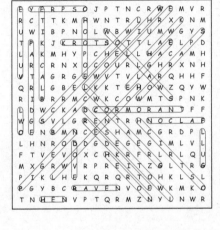

Word Search No. 50
Parts of the Body

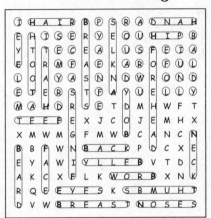

Word Search No. 51
Spices of the Bible

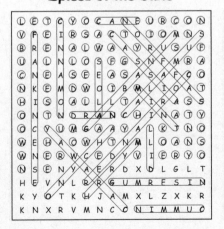

Word Search No. 52
Myrrh

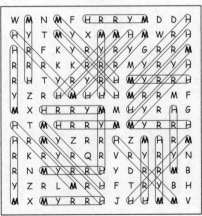

Word Search No. 53

Plants of the Bible

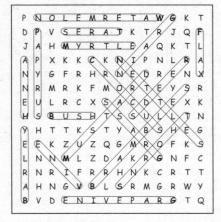

Word Search No. 54

Animals/Creeping Things

Word Search No. 55

More Parts of the Body

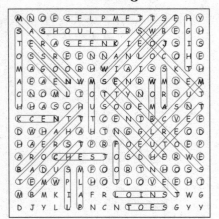

Word Search No. 56

Insects of the Bible

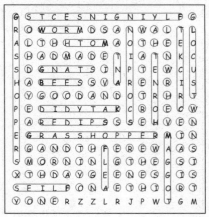

Word Search No. 57
Trees of the Bible

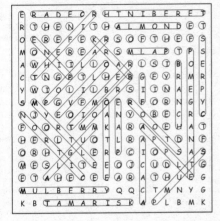

Word Search No. 58
Locusts and Wild Honey

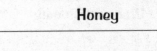
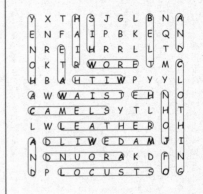

Word Search No. 59
More Edibles

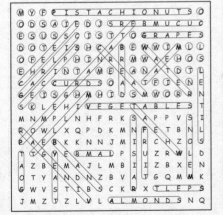

Word Search No. 60
Natural Phenomena: Earth

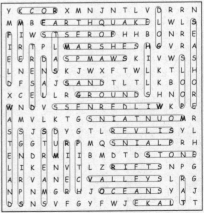

Word Search No. 61

Precious Stones

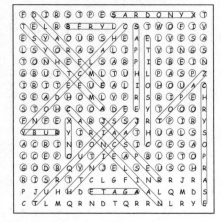

Word Search No. 62

Mountains of the Bible

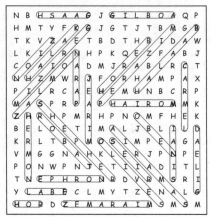

Word Search No. 63

Nature's Joy

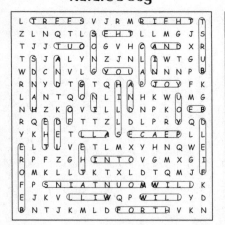

Word Search No. 64

Rivers of the Bible

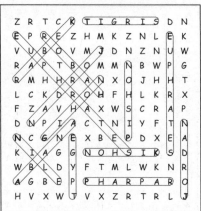

Word Search No. 65

Lights and Shadows

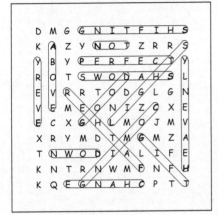

Word Search No. 66

Natural Phenomena: From Above

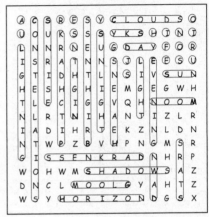

Word Search No. 67

Jerusalem

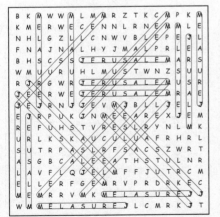

Word Search No. 68

Natural Phenomena: Weather

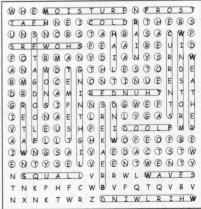

Word Search No. 69

Provinces

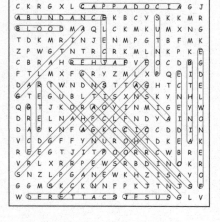

Word Search No. 70

Cities and Villages

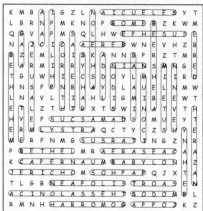

Word Search No. 71

Redemption

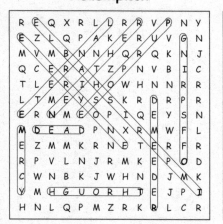

Word Search No. 72

Joy

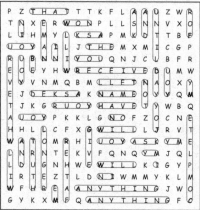

Word Search No. 73

Eternal Life

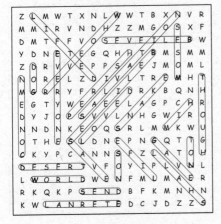

Word Search No. 74

New Birth

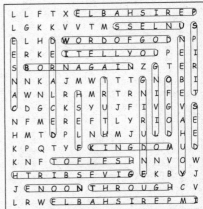

Word Search No. 75

Member of God's Household

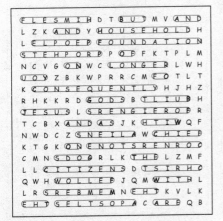

Word Search No. 76

Justification

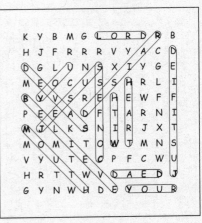

Word Search No. 77

Heaven

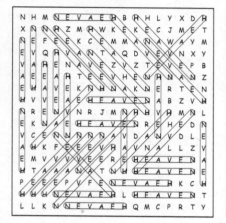

Word Search No. 78

Salvation's Gifts

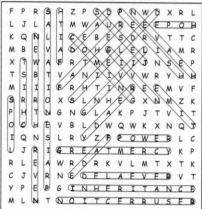

Word Search No. 79

Temples Not Built with Hands

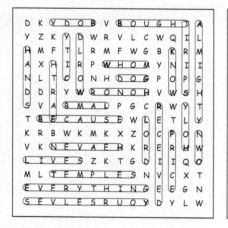

Word Search No. 80

Salvation

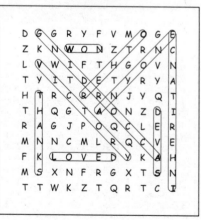

Word Search No. 81
Faith

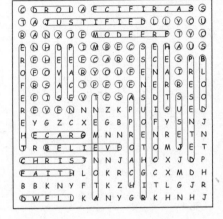

Word Search No. 82
Grace

Word Search No. 83
Heroes of Faith

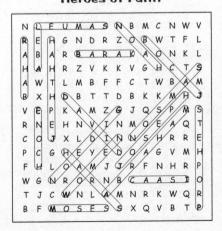

Word Search No. 84
Daniel and Friends

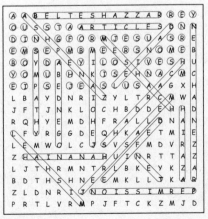

Word Search No. 85

New Testament Women

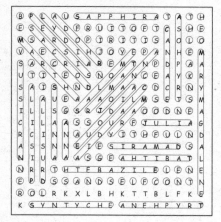

Word Search No. 86

Prophet

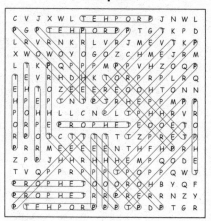

Word Search No. 87

Ruth's Decision

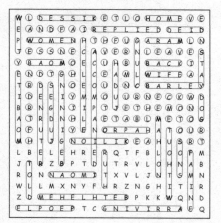

Word Search No. 88

Bible Couples

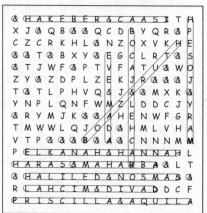

Word Search No. 89
The Kings of Judah

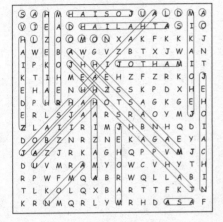

Word Search No. 90
Ruth's Dependence

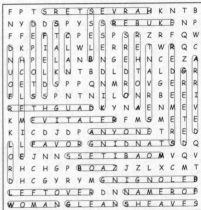

Word Search No. 91
The Noble Bereans

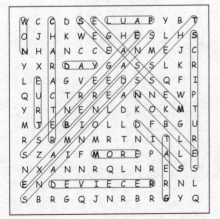

Word Search No. 92
Zacchaeus' Determination

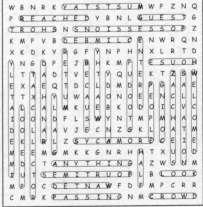

Word Search No. 93
Paul's Conversion

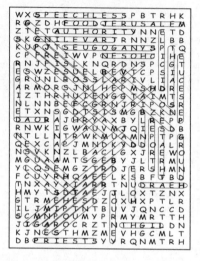

Word Search No. 94
Family

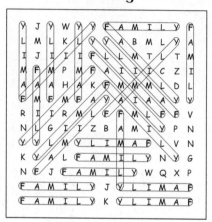

Word Search No. 95
Timothy

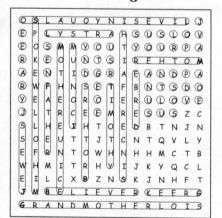

Word Search No. 96
Ruth's Delight

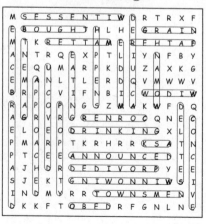

Answers to Fill-Ins

2. 5, 12, 8, 7, 10, 9, 19, 20, 4, 25, 24, 23, 26, 3, 2, 1, 22, 21, 18, 11, 27, 6, 14, 13, 16, 15, 17

5. 66

6. 8, 9, 16, 12, 10, 13, 1, 2, 6, 7, 11, 15, 14, 3, 4, 5, 17

7.
10:7	gate, sheep
10:11	shepherd
11:25	resurrection
12:26	servant
13:13	teacher, Lord
13:19	telling
14:2	prepare
14:3	where
14:6	way, truth, life
14:11	Father
14:12	going
15:1	true, vine
16:5	sent
16:28	leaving
18:37	king
19:28	thirsty
20:17	returning
20:21	sending

10.
1. Adam	Genesis 1:26,28; 2:20	
2. Bible	Holy Bible, New International Version, Preface	
3. David	Samuel 17:4,50	
4. Eve	Genesis 3:20	
5. John	Holy Bible, New International Version, introduction to the Book of John	
6. Mary	Luke 2:16,21	
7. Moses	Exodus 2:3-9	
8. Noah	Genesis 6:13-14	
9. Samson	Judges 16:6	
10. 39		
11. 27		
12. 50		
13. 4		
14. 31		
15. 28		
16. Daniel	Daniel 6:16	
17. Peter	Matthew 14:29	
18. Esther		
19. Solomon	1 Kings 3:1	
20. Judas	John 18:2	

12. Exodus
Numbers
Joshua
Ruth
Nehemiah
Job
Proverbs
Song of Songs
Jeremiah
Lamentations
Hosea

Amos
Jonah
Nahum
Zephaniah
Malachi
Matthew
Luke
Acts
Galatians
Philippians
Titus
Hebrews
Jude

14. 50

16.
1:1	beginning
1:3	fellowship
1:5	message
1:7	light
1:9	confess, faithful, unrighteousness
2:1	children, anybody, speaks
2:15	world, anything
2:20	anointing
2:25	eternal

17. Major Prophets: 5, 4, 1, 2, 3
Minor Prophets: 8, 13, 15, 6, 7, 10, 17, 11, 12, 9, 16, 14

19.
3:1	lavished, know
3:9	born
3:11	love
3:16	laid
3:20	everything
3:23	believe
4:1	false
4:4	overcome
4:10	sacrifice
4:14	Savior
4:18	fear
5:4	victory
5:12	life
5:21	idols

20.
1.	Mary	Matthew 1:18
2.	Joseph	Matthew 1:20
3.	wine	John 2:9
4.	water	John 2:9
5.	three	John 19:18
6.	true	John 19:18
7.	Paul	Acts 13:9
8.	Luke	Luke, Introduction
9.	Jude	Holy Bible, New International Version, Contents
10.	Luke	Colossians 4:14
11.	Ruth	Holy Bible, New International Version, Contents
12.	Peter	Matthew 14:29

22. Genesis
Leviticus
Deuteronomy
Judges
Ezra
Esther
Psalms
Ecclesiastes
Isaiah

Ezekiel
Daniel
Joel
Obadiah
Micah
Habakkuk
Haggai
Zechariah
Mark
John
Romans
Ephesians
Colossians
Philemon
James

25. 1:1   God, earth
    1:2   formless, darkness, hovering
    1:3   light
    1:4   separated
    1:5   day, evening, morning
    1:6   expanse, separate
    1:7   water
    1:8   sky, second
    1:9   gathered, ground
    1:10 land, seas
    1:11 produce, plants, various

27. 19

29. 1:14-15   lights, day, night, seasons, years
    1:16   greater, govern, lesser, stars
    1:17-18   earth, good
    1:19   evening, fourth

    1:20   water, creatures, birds, across
    1:21   created, living, moving, teems, winged, according
    1:22   fruitful, number, increase

31. 40

32. 1. armor
    2. helmet
    3. javelin
    4. sword
    5. archers
    6. spear
    7. arrow
    8. chariots
    9. bows
    10 . horse
    11. fortress
    12. shields
    13. noise
    14. club
    15. quiver
    16. cavalry
    17 . light
    18. trumpet
    19. righteousness
    20. truth
    21. salvation
    22. spirit
    23. faith

35. 1:24   produce, kinds, livestock, wild
    1:25   animals, along

1:26   man, likeness, over, fish, air, move

1:27   image, male, female

1:28   blessed, fill, subdue, rule

1:29   bearing, face, whole, tree, food

1:30   beasts, everything, green

42. 25

52. 30

61. 1. ruby, topaz, emerald, chrysolite, onyx, jasper, sapphire, turquoise, beryl

    2. chalcedony

    3. sardonyx, carnelian, chrysoprase, jacinth, amethyst

    4. agate

62. Olives, John 8:1

    Sinai, Acts 7:3

    Zion, Revelation 14:1

64.
Genesis 2:11	Pishon
Genesis 2:13	Gihon
Genesis 2:14	Tigris
Genesis 2:14	Euphrates
Genesis 15:18	Egypt
Joshua 4:7	Jordan
Judges 4:13	Kishon
2 Kings 5:12	Abana
2 Kings 5:12	Pharpar
2 Kings 17:6	Habor
Isaiah 19:7	Nile
Ezekiel 3:15	Kebar
Mark 1:5	Jordan
Revelation 16:12	Euphrates

67. 22

71. **R**edeemed

    Eternal

    Dead

    Everyone

    Mercy

    Purpose

    Through

    Imperishable

    Offspring

    Neither

77. 35

80. **S**aved

    Anyone

    Loved

    Victory

    According

    Thanks

    Inheritance

    Other

    Now

84.
1:1	Jehoiakim
1:1	Nebuchadnezzar
1:1	Jerusalem
1:2	articles
1:3	Ashpenaz
1:6	1) Daniel
	2) Hananiah
	3) Mishael
	4) Azariah
1:7	1) Belteshazzar
	2) Shadrach
	3) Meshach
	4) Abednego

	1:8	defile
	1:8	permission
	1:9	sympathy
	1:12	ten
86.	30	
87.	1:1	judges, famine, Bethlehem, wife, sons, Moab
	1:2	Elimelech, Naomi, Mahlon, Kilion
	1:3-4	died, Moabite, Orpah, Ruth
	1:5	without
	1:7-8	Judah, back, home
	1:14	wept, kissed, clung
	1:16	replied, stay, people, God
	1:19	women
	1:20	told, Mara
	1:22	returned, accompanied, arriving, barley, beginning
90.	2:1	relative, Elimelech, standing, Boaz
	2:2	Moabitess, fields, leftover, anyone, favor

	2:3	glean, harvesters, found, belonging, clan
	2:4	arrived, greeted, Lord, bless
	2:5	foreman, woman
	2:8	daughter, another, servant
	2:15	orders, sheaves
	2:16	stalks, rebuke
	2:20	stopped, kindness, redeemers
94.	24	
96.	3:1-2	provided, winnowing
	3:7-9	eating, drinking, grain, approached, uncovered, middle, woman, corner, garment
	3:11	ask, townsmen
	3:18	happens, matter, settled
	4:9	announced, witnesses, bought, property
	4:10	acquired, widow, disappear
	4:13	became, conceive
	4:17	Obed, father

Hidden Messages List

[Note: Bracketed references are not part of hidden messages.]

1. "This is the day the LORD has made; let us rejoice and be glad in it." [Psalm 118:24]

3. You are precious to the Lord Jesus.

8. "Looking unto Jesus, the author and finisher of our faith." [Hebrews 12:2 KJV]

9. Let Jesus come into your heart.

10. "For Ezra had devoted himself to the study and observance of the law of the Lord, and to teaching its decrees and laws in Israel." Ezra seven:ten

13. "In all your ways acknowledge him, and he will make your paths straight." Proverbs three:six

16. "In the beginning God created the heavens and the earth." He also made the stars. [Genesis 1:1]

18. Do you know that Jesus loves you?

19. "In all your ways acknowledge him, and he will make your paths straight." [Proverbs 3:6]

30. "This is the victory that has overcome the world, even our faith." [1 John 5:4]

34. With Christ you will have victory. Just leave the battle to Him.

36. "For everyone born of God overcomes the world." [1 John 5:4]

37. "I have set my rainbow in the clouds, and it will be the sign of the covenant between me and the earth." [Genesis 9:13]

39. "Let us come before him with thanksgiving and extol him with music and song." [Psalm 95:2]

41. "Create in me a pure heart." [Psalm 51:10]

43. "But those sacrifices are an annual reminder of sins, because it is impossible for the blood of bulls and goats to take away sins." Hebrews ten:three

44. "Sing and make music in your heart to the Lord." [Ephesians 5:19]

45. What are you doing for Jesus?

47. Genesis two:twenty: "So the man gave names to all the livestock, the birds of the air and all the beasts of the field."

48. provision

50. "I praise you because I am fearfully and wonderfully made." [Psalm 139:14]

51. "Let your conversation be always full of grace seasoned with salt, so that you may know how to answer everyone." [Colossians 4:6]

53. watermelon

55. "No eye has seen, no ear has heard, no mind has conceived what God has prepared for those who love him." [1 Corinthians 2:9]

56. "God saw all that he had made and it was very good. And there was evening and there was morning the—sixth day." Genesis one:thirty-one

57. "Then the trees of the forest will sing, they will sing for joy before the LORD for he comes to judge the earth." [1 Chronicles 16:33]

59. "'My food,' said Jesus, 'is to do the will of him who sent me and to finish his work.'" [John 4:34]

61. First Peter two:five "Yourselves also, as living stones, are being built up a spiritual house, a holy priesthood, to offer spiritual sacrifices acceptable to God by Jesus Christ." [DARBY]

66. Are you shining for Jesus?

68. "When neither sun nor stars appeared for many days and the storm continued raging, we finally gave up all hope of being saved." Acts twenty-seven:twenty

73. salvation

81. "Cast all your anxiety on him because he cares for you." First Peter five:seven

84. Are you standing for Jesus? Remember, somebody loves you. His name is Jesus.

85. "But the fruit of the spirit is love, joy, peace, patience, kindness, goodness, faithfulness, gentleness and self-control." [Galatians 5:22-23]

87. "Let love and faithfulness never leave you; bind them around your neck, write them on the tablet of your heart." [Proverbs 3:3]

89. Saul, David, Solomon [1 Samuel 11:15; 1 Chronicles 12:38; 1 Kings 5:12]

95. Jesus loves you, your parents, and grandparents. Do you love Jesus?

Scripture References for Word-List Word Searches

Abijah	2 Chronicles 13:1	Baalah	Joshua 15:11
Abraham & Sarah	Genesis 18:11	baboons	2 Chronicles 9:21
acacia	Isaiah 41:19	Babylon	Revelation 18:21
Adam & Eve	Genesis 3:20	back	Exodus 33:23
Adoniram	1 Kings 5:14	bark	Genesis 30:37
adorned	2 Chronicles 3:6	barley (WS #48)	John 6:9
Ahaz	2 Chronicles 28:1	barley (WS #53)	Job 31:40
Ahaziah	2 Chronicles 22:1	baths	2 Chronicles 4:5
algum	2 Chronicles 2:8	bats	Isaiah 2:20
almond	Genesis 30:37	beans	Ezekiel 4:9
almonds	Genesis 43:11	bear	1 Samuel 17:36
aloes	Psalm 45:8	beard	Psalm 133:2
Amaziah	2 Chronicles 25:1	beast	Zechariah 8:10
Amon	2 Chronicles 33:21	beaten gold	1 Kings 6:32
ankles	Acts 3:7	Beersheba	2 Chronicles 30:5
Anna	Luke 2:36	bees	Judges 14:8
Anointed One	Daniel 9:25	Beginning	
ant	Proverbs 6:6	and the End	Revelation 22:13
antelope	Deuteronomy 14:5	bells	Exodus 28:35
apes	1 Kings 10:22	belly	Job 40:16
apostle	Hebrews 3:1	Berea	Acts 17:10
apple	Joel 1:12	Bethany	Luke 19:29
Araunah	2 Chronicles 3:1	Bethel	Genesis 12:8
archer	Jeremiah 51:3	Bethlehem	Luke 2:4
arms	Luke 15:20	black	Zechariah 6:6
army	Ezekiel 26:7	black kite	Deuteronomy
arrows	2 Samuel 11:24		14:13
articles	2 Chronicles 4:16	blacksmith	Isaiah 54:16
artisans	Jeremiah 24:1	black vulture	Leviticus 11:13
Asa	1 Kings 15:9	blessed and	
Asaph	1 Chronicles 15:19	only Ruler	1 Timothy 6:15
Ashkelon	Judges 1:18	blood	1 Peter 1:19
Athaliah	2 Kings 11:3	blue	2 Chronicles 3:14
attendant	Acts 13:7	boards	1 Kings 6:16
author	Hebrews 12:2	Boaz & Ruth	Ruth 4:13

counselors	Ezra 4:5
countrymen	Jeremiah 22:13
courtyard	2 Chronicles 4:9
Covenant for the people	Isaiah 42:6
covered	2 Chronicles 3:5
cow	Isaiah 11:7
craftsmen	Hosea 13:2
cream	Job 20:17
cricket	Leviticus 11:22
crimson	2 Chronicles 3:14
crocus	Isaiah 35:1
cubits	2 Chronicles 3:3
cucumbers	Numbers 11:5
cummin	Matthew 23:23
curds	2 Samuel 17:29
currents	Jonah 2:3
curtain	2 Chronicles 3:14
cymbals	1 Chronicles 15:28
cypress	Isaiah 41:19
Damaris	Acts 17:34
Damascus	Acts 22:10
dance	Job 21:11
dappled	Zechariah 6:6
dark	Genesis 30:32
darkness	Isaiah 59:9
dart	Job 41:26
dates	2 Samuel 6:19
David	1 Samuel 16:23
David & Michal	1 Samuel 18:27
dawn	Matthew 28:1
day	Psalm 139:12
dealer in purple	Acts 16:14
death	Psalm 116:15
decorated	2 Chronicles 3:5
decorating	2 Chronicles 4:12
deer	Deuteronomy 14:5
Derbe	Acts 14:6

desert	Acts 8:26
desert owl	Leviticus 11:18
designers	Exodus 35:35
designs	2 Chronicles 3:5
dew	Deuteronomy 33:13
dill	Matthew 23:23
dishes	2 Chronicles 4:22
dog	Proverbs 26:17
donkey	2 Peter 2:16
Dorcas	Acts 9:36
dove	Psalm 68:13
dragon	Revelation 20:2
Drusilla	Acts 24:24
eagle	Leviticus 11:13
earthquake	Acts 16:26
Ebal	Joshua 8:30
Elizabeth	Luke 1:5
Elkanah & Hannah	1 Samuel 1:8
embroiderer	Exodus 27:16
engravers	2 Chronicles 2:7
Ephesus	Acts 19:1
Ephron	Joshua 15:9
equipment	1 Samuel 8:12
Euodia	Philippians 4:2
evangelist	Acts 21:8
evening	Luke 21:37
Everlasting Father	Isaiah 9:6
everlasting light	Isaiah 60:20
eye	Matthew 6:22
eyebrows	Leviticus 14:9
eyes	1 John 1:1
face	Job 29:24
faith	2 Peter 1:1
Faithful and True	Revelation 19:11
faithful and true witness	Revelation 3:14

faithful witness	Revelation 1:5	gate	John 10:9
falcon	Deuteronomy 14:13	gatekeepers	1 Chronicles 9:26
farmer	James 5:7	Gaza	Acts 8:26
feet	1 Corinthians 15:25	gazelle	Proverbs 6:5
field	1 Peter 1:24	gecko	Leviticus 11:30
fig	Joel 1:12	Gerizim	Deuteronomy 27:12
fighting men	Joshua 1:14	gift	Genesis 30:20
figs	Numbers 13:23	Gilboa	2 Samuel 1:6
figures	2 Chronicles 4:3	Gilead	Judges 7:3
fine linen	2 Chronicles 3:14	gloom	Hebrews 12:18
fingers	Mark 7:33	gnats	Exodus 8:17
fish	Numbers 11:5	goat	Judges 6:19
flaming torches	Isaiah 50:11	gold	1 Peter 1:18 (WS #3),
flax	Exodus 9:31	Genesis 2:11	
flea	1 Samuel 24:14	golden altar	2 Chronicles 4:19
fleet	Daniel 11:40	gold nails	2 Chronicles 3:9
flies	Exodus 8:24	goldsmiths	Nehemiah 3:31
float	1 Kings 5:9	Gomorrah	Genesis 19:24
flood	Genesis 9:11	good shepherd	John 10:11
floodgates	Genesis 7:11	gourds	1 Kings 6:18
floral work	2 Chronicles 4:21	governors	Ezekiel 23:6
flour	Revelation 18:13	grain	1 Timothy 5:18
flute	Daniel 3:5	grapes	Numbers 13:23
flying insects	Deuteronomy 14:19	grapevine	James 3:12
foot	Proverbs 25:19	grass	Numbers 22:4
foot soldiers	1 Chronicles 18:4	grasshopper	Leviticus 11:22
forehead	Isaiah 48:4	grasshoppers	Isaiah 40:22
foremen	1 Kings 5:16	gray	Proverbs 20:29
forests	Isaiah 44:23	great owl	Leviticus 11:17
fowl	1 Kings 4:23	great Shepherd	Hebrews 13:20
fox	Nehemiah 4:3	green	Mark 6:39
frankincense	Revelation 18:13	ground	Exodus 9:23
frogs	Psalm 78:45	gull	Leviticus 11:16
frost	Psalm 147:16	gum resin	Exodus 30:34
fruit	Ezekiel 34:27	hail	Exodus 9:23
furnishings	2 Chronicles 5:1	hair	John 12:3
Gaash	Joshua 24:30	Halak	Joshua 12:7
galbanum	Exodus 30:34	hand	1 Corinthians 12:21
garlic	Numbers 11:5	handbreadth	2 Chronicles 4:5

harpists	Revelation 18:22
harps	1 Chronicles 15:28
haul	1 Kings 5:9
hawk	Leviticus 11:16
heart	Hebrews 4:12
heat	James 1:11
heavens	Genesis 7:19
heifer	Genesis 15:9
helmets	Ezekiel 23:24
Heman	1 Chronicles 6:33
hen	Luke 13:34
henna	Song of Songs 1:14
Hermon	Joshua 11:17
heron	Leviticus 11:19
Hezekiah	2 Chronicles 29:1
hills	Matthew 18:12
hindquarters	2 Chronicles 4:4
hip	Genesis 32:32
Hiram	1 Kings 5:7
hired worker	Leviticus 25:6
honey	Deuteronomy 31:20
hoopoe	Leviticus 11:19
Hor	Numbers 20:27
Horeb	Exodus 33:6
horizon	Job 26:10
horn	Daniel 3:5
horned owl	Leviticus 11:16
hornet	Exodus 23:28
horse	1 Kings 20:25
horseman	Amos 2:15
horsemen	Ezekiel 26:7
horses	Isaiah 22:6
Hosanna	Mark 11:9
Huram	1 Kings 7:14
hyenas	Isaiah 34:14
hymns	Colossians 3:16
I AM	Exodus 3:14
ibex	Deuteronomy 14:5
Iconium	2 Timothy 3:11

instruments	Amos 6:5
interwoven	2 Chronicles 3:16
iron workers	2 Chronicles 24:12
Isaac & Rebekah	Genesis 24:67
Israel	Isaiah 43:1,3
jackal	Micah 1:8
Jacob	Isaiah 43:1,4
javelins	2 Samuel 18:14
Jearim	Joshua 15:10
Jebusite	2 Chronicles 3:1
Jehoiachin	2 Chronicles 36:9
Jehoiakim	2 Chronicles 36:5
Jehoram	2 Chronicles 21:5
Jehoshaphat	1 Kings 22:2
Jericho	Hebrews 11:30
Jerusalem	Acts 21:31
jewel	Revelation 21:11
Joanna	Luke 8:3
Joash	2 Chronicles 24:1
joints	Hebrews 4:12
Joppa	Jonah 1:3
Josiah	2 Chronicles 34:1
Jotham	2 Chronicles 27:1
Jubal	Genesis 4:21
judge	Isaiah 3:2
Judge of all the earth	Genesis 18:25
Julia	Romans 16:15
katydid	Leviticus 11:22
King	Jeremiah 23:5
King of glory	Psalm 24:10
King of heaven	Daniel 4:37
King of Israel	John 1:49
King of kings	Revelation 17:14
King of the ages	Revelation 15:3
King of the Jews	John 19:21
knees	Isaiah 35:3
laborers	1 Kings 5:13
lake	Matthew 8:24

nard	Mark 14:3	partridge	Jeremiah 17:11
Nazareth	Matthew 2:23	pearls	Revelation 17:4
Neapolis	Acts 16:11	Perazim	Isaiah 28:21
Nebo	Deuteronomy 34:1	Persis	Romans 16:12
neck	Genesis 33:4	Philippi	Mark 8:27
nettles	Isaiah 34:13	pig	Leviticus 11:7
night	Genesis 1:5	pigeon	Genesis 15:9
Nineveh	Jonah 3:3	pine	Hosea 14:8
no chisel	1 Kings 6:7	pine logs	1 Kings 5:8
no hammer	1 Kings 6:7	pipes	Daniel 3:5
no iron tool	1 Kings 6:7	pistachio nuts	Genesis 43:11
nose	Song of Songs 7:4	pitch	Exodus 2:3
noses	Psalm 115:6	pitch dark	Amos 5:20
oak tree	1 Kings 13:14	plains	Numbers 22:1
oceans	Proverbs 8:24	plane	Genesis 30:37
officers	2 Chronicles 21:9	polished bronze	2 Chronicles 4:16
oil	Psalm 133:2	pomegranate	Joel 1:12
olive (WS #48)	Habakkuk 3:17	pomegranates	2 Chronicles 3:16
olive (WS #57)	Romans 11:24	pools	Psalm 107:35
olive oil	Revelation 18:13	poplar	Genesis 30:37
olive wood	1 Kings 6:23	pots	2 Chronicles 4:11
Olives	John 8:1	precious stones	2 Chronicles 3:6
onions	Numbers 11:5	priests	2 Chronicles 4:9
onycha	Exodus 30:34	Priscilla	Acts 18:2
onyx	Job 28:16	Priscilla & Aquila	Acts 18:2
open flowers	1 Kings 6:18	promises	2 Peter 1:4
osprey	Deuteronomy 14:17	psalms	Colossians 3:16
ostrich	Job 39:13	pure gold	2 Chronicles 3:4
overlaid	2 Chronicles 3:4	purple	2 Chronicles 2:7
owl	Isaiah 34:15	quail	Psalm 105:40
oxen	Luke 14:19	quarry	1 Kings 5:17
pale	Revelation 6:8	rabbit	Leviticus 11:6
palm (WS #55)	Leviticus 14:17	Rachel & Jacob	Genesis 29:28
palm (WS #57)	Joel 1:12	rafts	2 Chronicles 2:16
palm tree	2 Chronicles 3:5	rain	James 5:18
Paphos	Acts 13:6	rainbow	Revelation 4:3
papyrus	Exodus 2:3	raisins	2 Samuel 6:19
Paran	Habakkuk 3:3	ram	Leviticus 5:15

ram's horns	1 Chronicles 15:28	shovels	2 Chronicles 4:11
rat	Leviticus 11:29	showers	Zechariah 10:1
raven	Leviticus 11:15	Sidon	Joel 3:4
red	Isaiah 1:18	Sidonians	1 Chronicles 22:4
red kite	Deuteronomy 14:13	siege ramp	Isaiah 37:33
reeds	Exodus 2:3	silver	1 Peter 1:18
Rehoboam	1 Kings 12:17	Sinai	Acts 7:30
Rhoda	Acts 12:13	sinews	Isaiah 48:4
rifts	Jeremiah 2:6	singers	1 Chronicles 15:27
river	Acts 16:13	sistrums	2 Samuel 6:5
rock	1 Peter 2:8	skink	Leviticus 11:30
roe	Deuteronomy 14:5	sky	Matthew 16:2-3
Rome	Acts 23:11	sling stones	1 Chronicles 12:2
roots	Job 18:16	snake	John 3:14
rubies	Proverbs 8:11	snow	Psalm 147:16
saffron	Song of Songs 4:14	socket	Genesis 32:32
Salamis	Acts 13:5	sockets	1 Kings 6:34
Salome	Mark 16:1	Sodom	Genesis 19:24
salt (WS #48)	Colossians 4:6	solid gold	2 Chronicles 4:21
salt (WS #60)	James 3:11	song	Exodus 15:1
Samaria	Amos 6:1	songs	Colossians 3:16
Samson & Delilah	Judges 16:3-4	sons	Lamentations 4:2
sand	Jeremiah 33:22	Sovereign Lord	Revelation 6:10
Sapphira	Acts 5:1	sow	2 Peter 2:22
sapphires	Job 28:16	sparrow	Psalm 84:3
scarlet	Isaiah 1:18	spears	Nahum 2:3
scorpion	Revelation 9:5	speckled	Genesis 30:32
screech owl	Leviticus 11:16	spelt	Ezekiel 4:9
sculptured	2 Chronicles 3:10	spices	Psalm 75:8
seashore	Hebrews 11:12	spider	Job 8:14
Seir	Joshua 15:10	spotted	Genesis 30:32
Seleucia	Acts 13:4	springs	Isaiah 41:18
serpent	Isaiah 27:1	sprinkling bowls	2 Chronicles 4:8
shadows	Isaiah 59:9	squall	Mark 4:37
sheep	Acts 8:32	stag	Song of Songs 2:9
shekels	2 Chronicles 3:9	stars	Psalm 8:3
Shepher	Numbers 33:24	steeds	Jeremiah 47:3
ships	Daniel 11:40	stomach	Luke 15:16
shoulder	Genesis 24:46	stone (WS #38)	2 Kings 22:6

stone (WS #60)	1 Peter 2:8
stonecutters	1 Chronicles 22:2
stones	Exodus 28:17
stork	Leviticus 11:19
streams	Isaiah 34:9
strings	Psalm 45:8
stump	Job 14:8
sun	1 Corinthians 15:41
sunlight	Isaiah 30:26
sunrise	Mark 16:2
Susanna	Luke 8:3
swallow	Psalm 84:3
swamps	Ezekiel 47:11
sycamore	Luke 19:4
Sychar	John 4:5
Syntyche	Philippians 4:2
Tabitha	Acts 9:36
tables	2 Chronicles 4:8
Tabor	Judges 4:14
talents	2 Chronicles 3:8
Tamar	Matthew 1:3
tamarisk	Genesis 21:33
tambourines	1 Chronicles 13:8
tar	Exodus 2:3
tares	Matthew 13:30 KJV
Tarsus	Acts 21:39
teams	Isaiah 21:7
teeth	Jeremiah 31:29
tempest	Psalm 107:25
temples	Song of Songs 4:3
ten basins	2 Chronicles 4:6
tendon	Genesis 32:32
terebinth	Hosea 4:13
the fir	Isaiah 41:19
Thessalonica	Acts 17:1
thigh	Exodus 28:42
things	Ezekiel 22:25
this stone	1 Peter 2:7
thorns	Isaiah 7:25

thoughts	Psalm 139:17
throat	Jeremiah 2:25
thumb	Leviticus 14:17
thumbs	Exodus 29:20
thunder	Exodus 9:23
Tiberias	John 6:23
timber (WS #38)	1 Kings 5:6
timber (WS #57)	2 Chronicles 2:8
toes	Exodus 29:20
tongs	2 Chronicles 4:21
tongue	James 1:26
tooth	Proverbs 25:19
trap	Jeremiah 50:24
Troas	Acts 16:11
troops	2 Chronicles 12:3
trumpet	Zechariah 9:14
trumpeters	Revelation 18:22
trumpets	1 Chronicles 15:28
Tryphena	Romans 16:12
Tryphosa	Romans 16:12
twelve bulls	2 Chronicles 4:4
Tyre	Joel 3:4
Uzziah	2 Chronicles 26:1
valleys	Isaiah 41:18
vegetables	Romans 14:2
vine	John 15:4
vinegar	Ruth 2:14
vipers	Psalm 140:3
voice	Judges 5:11
vulture	Leviticus 11:13
wages	1 Kings 5:6
wagons	Ezekiel 23:24
waist	Jeremiah 13:1
wall lizard	Leviticus 11:30
war clubs	Ezekiel 39:9
war horses	Ezekiel 26:10
wasteland	Isaiah 43:19
water	John 4:13
waves	Psalm 42:7

weapons	Ezekiel 23:24	wolf	Isaiah 65:25
weasel	Leviticus 11:29	womb	Luke 1:44
weather	Matthew 16:2	word of God	Ephesians 6:17
wheat	Revelation 18:13	workmen	1 Kings 5:16
whirlwind	Nahum 1:3	worm	Jonah 4:7
white	Isaiah 1:18	yarn	2 Chronicles 3:14
white owl	Leviticus 11:18	yeast	Galatians 5:9
wick trimmers	2 Chronicles 4:22	yellow	Revelation 9:17
wilderness	Isaiah 35:6	you	Isaiah 43:4
wild goat	Deuteronomy 14:5	Zalmon	Judges 9:48
wind	James 1:6	Zedekiah	2 Chronicles 36:11
windstorm	Ezekiel 1:4	Zemaraim	2 Chronicles 13:4
wine	Luke 7:33	Zion	Revelation 14:1
wingspan	2 Chronicles 3:11	zither	Daniel 3:5
wisdom	Proverbs 8:11		

For Bible stories and more puzzles,
visit our Website

www.SearchtheWord.net

and click on "Fun Stuff."

You may contact us at
info@searchtheword.net.